THE CAKE LADY-

MY LIFE IN THE MIX

MIXING LIFE'S INGREDIENTS FOR SUCCESS

by

Diane "THE CAKE LADY"

DPW Publishing

Copyright 2021

ISBN 978-1-7376943-0-4

TABLE OF CONTENTS

PREFACE

Acknowledgments

Mixing Life's Ingredients for Success

PREFACE

Several years ago, I was going through my closet getting rid of clothes and shoes when I came across all kinds of old journals and calendars. This included memos, dates, and memorable times from the past 45 years of my life. I thought for a moment that I should get rid of it but after reading through some of the pages, I thought: "I should write a book."

My life has been marbled with so many different experiences and I thought that maybe, just maybe, something in it could inspire someone else. Possibly, the problems I encountered during my journey, others may be able to relate to and find it helpful in working through their own crises. My story may inspire a child who's been hurt or the new entrepreneur struggling to get started or help someone feel like they are not the only one with relationship issues. I knew I had God's Grace all over me—even when I strayed, did not pray, and wanted to do things my way.

God's purpose was in me. So, I started writing and stringing events together to put the pieces in place. I found myself crying, screaming, shaking my head, and laughing out loud at the unbelievable, sad, hilarious, scary, and exciting memories. It has taken a couple of years to get this into manuscript form and I hope that what you read will inspire you. There are many stories in everyone's lives that, if shared, could possibly make a difference in someone else's journey. It could be an intimidating experience exposing your heart and life to others. For me, it has proven to be therapeutic. Pouring my life into these pages has truly relieved me and allowed me to forgive, forget, and not forget some things but to grow from them.

Hopefully, my story will resonate with you and motivate you to share yours.

ACKNOWLEDGMENTS

In loving dedication to:

First and foremost, to God Almighty, for breathing life into me and ordering my steps. Thank you, Lord, for All of my many Blessings and your Grace and Mercy

My mom, for giving birth to me and believing in me no matter what I did, right or wrong

My two daughters, for putting up with me throughout their lives and during the writing of this book

The many mentors, who provided me with love, guidance, and support during the rough times and helped to usher me into the light of a fulfilling life.

My friend, Linda Richardson, editor, and embellisher of this book. She helped to transform my mess of scattered notes and memories into a masterpiece. This book would not be as well written if it was not for her.

My friends, neighbors, relatives, and customers, who pushed me to buy my own bakery and purchased enough product to fund it

.

My employees, who still manage to tolerate me—even when I drive them crazy.

My true and loyal friends (you know who you are), who believe in me and continue to stick by me to this day.

To Tracey Smith, Rosalia Scalia, Regina Davis, Tawanda Prince, and Patti McDermott for all their help, guidance and support.

To Elizabeth Thomas, thanks for stepping up and designing the most awesome book cover ever.

"The names have been changed to protect the innocent."

Maxwell Smart

Chapter 1

DEVELOPING THE RECIPE

"Obstacles are the cost of greatness."

Robin Sharma

INTERRUPTIONS! Every day is never empty of distractions at the Kake Korner Bakery. Here I go again, allowing myself to lose focus from mixing different icings to refereeing a disagreement between staff, checking an order to ensure it is correct, and having to attend to one issue after another. Already, I am off my plan, which plucks my last nerve. At least it's not like yesterday, when first thing in the morning I get the dreaded phone call, "I'm sick, I can't come in." Which means I must get up earlier, rush to get ready, and fight the work traffic to make my usual breakfast run to Dunkin' Donuts for tea and a sandwich. Of all days, the order line is out of the driveway to the street.

Forget this! My "pissocity" meter rises another notch because not only do I have to fill in for an absent employee, but also miss my breakfast. The thought of having to be at work much earlier than planned puts me in stress mode. When I arrive at the bakery, I am told another employee will be late and another has also called out. Being short staffed now means that I, Diane, 'The Cake Lady,' a witty, workaholic business woman who has overcome hell and high water to own and operate a business with a crew of 14 still must deal with the one uncontrollable ever-present challenge of reliable staffing.

To begin the day and move through the fog of distractions, I put on my "work-out-front hat" and ready myself to cover for my absent salesgirl, then switch to my decorator hat for my absent decorator, and then put on my owner's hat to begin to tackle my paperwork. I am a hands-on, doing what I have to do to make it happen, woman, but the icing on this day's cake is that one customer who comes into the bakery (never been here before), surveys the area, and can't help but see me working my butt off. Smiling, I issue my customary cheerful greeting, which elicits the response, "Wow, it must be great working at something you are so passionate about." Passion is not what I am feeling right now; however, I have mastered how not to mirror a face that reflects what I am really feeling in the moment. I put on my big fake smile and answer "Yes, it's great." My response ushers me past the mood, take care of the customer's needs and keep going so I can get back to the mix. I keep my true feelings from spilling out and not tell her how today, the passion she thinks I have is as lumpy as the lumps in the cake batter that I should be working on. I kick into "survival mode" to juggle all the balls being thrown at me and it's only 10 a.m.

I wonder how many customers stopping in to pick up their order or design a cake see me as a successful entrepreneur and think to themselves, "Diane has got it made!" I often get questions like: How did you start your business? What has contributed to your success? Are you really the owner? How did you get interested in baking?

I must admit, after years of blood, sweat, and tears, I am grateful to God that the Kake Korner is still alive and thriving — a business I purchased not so much out of my passion for baking, but the need to pay my bills and survive.

After satisfying this patron's curiosity, I continue the business at hand, while reflecting on how all this "success" really came about. Truth be told, this memoir was written to share, especially with people who think they know me, the unimaginable lumps and broken eggshells mixed into the batter of my life. Some think it is all sparkles and glitter to own a bakery like Kake Korner. They see a premier bakery that produces creative custom cakes, and they happily drive away with their edible work of art, never knowing what goes on behind the scenes. Long before you get to the glitter, there is a lot of grunt work involved that nobody knows about.

My story is riddled with experiences that no one would believe I have been through. From the outside looking in, one may call it success based on what they see; however, my definition of success is how I have been able to overcome many of life's hurdles. As I say all the time, "Nothing but the Grace of God." His hand has been upon my life, blessing me with wisdom and strength all along the way and putting the right people in place to help me through the tough times.

INITIAL INGREDIENTS

ATTITUDE!!! As early as age two, attitude was one of the initial ingredients in the recipe of my life. "There goes Lil' Miss Independent," as I was often referred to by my mom and other adults. Even then, people could see my determination to get

what I wanted, how I wanted it, and when I wanted it! I was Lil'
Miss Independent: feisty, defiant, and courageous. When I think
about how strong I was then, I now realize how these
characteristics were ingredients for my future success.

Being independent at a young age does not necessarily mean
you're always in control. In baking, the sugar always rises to the
top; just as in life, the truth tends to eventually do the same.
Frequent flashbacks and dreams about my past, found me at age
56 finding out that my childhood innocence was stolen from me by
my next-door neighbor, Mr. George.

Mr. George was the father of my friend Donna, the husband of
Mrs. Bev, all friends of my family. No one would have suspected
that between the ages of three to seven, while being babysat, I was
being taken to Mr. George's bedroom, held down and assaulted in
ways I cannot clearly recall. Even now, dark spaces, harsh raspy
voices, weird laughter, or seeing old neighbors trigger flashbacks.
I understand why sexual abuse often goes unnoticed and
unreported because of the bond between the abuser, the victim,

and the victim's family.

When I was inside Mr. George's house, Donna would encourage me to play a game where she would hold me down and Mr. George would undress and fondle me. A lanky, humped back, sinister looking man with a long, ugly face topped with curly dark hair, he reminded me of Lurch on the TV show The Addams Family. He had a mocking, hideous laugh and always made what he was doing to me seem like a game, like everyday normal behavior between an adult and child. I didn't know any better. I remember Donna pressing my arms down over my head saying, "Be still, be still," as her dad did things to me. I would fall asleep until I was awakened fully dressed and sent home as if nothing happened.

Donna, whom I considered my friend, was a couple years older than me. She had a reputation and was considered "bad" by folks in our neighborhood. She was always in trouble and getting suspended from school, especially when she hung out with the tough girls. She cussed, talked back to her mom, would sneak

13

drinks from her dad's alcohol and smoked his cigarettes. My mom did not particularly like Donna but found it hard to keep two little girls apart who had forged a friendship. Donna presented two faces, one as my friend, the other acting like her dad's sex kitten. Her lack of personal hygiene, along with her long, dirty matted hair shouted that she seldom took showers. Donna was not ugly, but neither would I label her pretty; she was more of a plain Jane, country bumpkin who acted more like an adult. When I think back, I believe her not caring about how she looked or acted had something to do with her father, who was probably molesting her, too. Why else would she be a willing participant in what her dad was doing to me? Donna's mother, Ms. Bev, had little to say about how Donna acted or her neglected appearance. She reminded me of Edith, Archie Bunker's wife on the "All in the Family" TV show. To me, Miss Bev acted dumb like Edith because I believe she knew what her husband was doing to children, including their daughter. Could it be that he was also abusive to her, causing her to be fearful of the consequences if she said anything?

So many women have stayed quiet for so long. Now we have the "Me Too" movement empowering women to share their experiences and, hopefully, jail the perpetrators.

As I got older, when Donna wanted me to come over, my mother would not allow me anywhere near her. Her reputation of being too grown for her age and associating with the "wild" boys, caused my mother, as well as other mothers in the neighborhood, to forbid us from being around her. Their "mother sense," that nothing good would ever come of her, proved prophetic. I learned that later in her life she became a drug addict, had two children by two different fathers whom she abandoned, and tragically while drunk and high on drugs, walked out into the middle of a highway and was run over by a truck. Later, when I reflected on why, from ages 12 to 14, I acted out like Donna — promiscuous, defiant, a little Miss Know-it-All — I realized it was my way of getting attention and being seen and heard because of being molested. I was looking for love, or what I thought was love, in all the wrong places.

My behaviors over shadowed the good within me and were unknowingly a cry for help. As a child, I would cry myself to sleep at night. I felt different, empty, alone, and misunderstood. Feeling ashamed, embarrassed, and not knowing what was right or wrong, I was scared. Who could I trust? Who was going to hurt me next or blame me for something that was not my fault? I should've had someone to talk to about what was happening to me, but I was too young to know what to do.

It was evident that growing up in a middle-class, all-white neighborhood, stay-at-home mothers often yielded to the brash, arrogance of husbands and male rule. Women stayed in their place and men dominated their families. At an early age, I observed how wives catered to their husbands' every demand. To not comply with a husband's command would often initiate scenes of shouting, threatening language, and possible physical violence. There was a posture of timidity in how wives interacted with their husbands and male friends. Mothers were either naive to what the groping of their children by some men represented, or just chose not to address what they saw. I observed it happening to other girls and experienced it myself, how "familiar" men would get by putting their hands on us and rubbing our backsides while sitting us on their laps. There was one man who would lean in close to my face and stick his tongue in my ear, sometimes licking the side of my face as he thought this was cute. I really wanted to slap him. Some moms thought it was alright and even laughed about it. I continually wondered why they did not do something. It was gross. To tell my mom how I felt probably would not have made a difference, most likely being shrugged off as playful gestures. Talking about sex or a child being inappropriately touched or molested back then was taboo. I concluded that mothers thought it was cute when men groped their daughters, maybe because it was that way when they were growing up.

PARENTS: Please pay attention when your child acts out or says they are uncomfortable being around anyone: male or female, relative or not.

Children have an internal sense that should be believed. Protect them! They need to feel safe!!

For the victim, time never erases the damage done to the soul, the hurt to the heart or the caring thoughts for others. Even now when children are in the bakery showroom or when I speak to students at local schools, my mind tends to wonder how many of them have been victimized.

LINE UP THE REST

I was a tall "girlie girl" five-year-old kindergartener, with long pigtails who was headstrong about everything and afraid of nothing. An incident of how I could hold my own involved one of my kindergarten classmates, a tall, husky, blond-haired boy whose teeth were so messed up, you hated for him to open his mouth. He was bigger than all the students in the class. Whenever we had to form a line, he would always get behind me and pull on my pigtails. I asked him nicely several times to stop pulling my hair and after letting him bully me far too long, I knew I had to stand up to him. Having had enough, I kicked him in the shin, HARD! As is the case with some bullies, he got all "sissified" and started crying. I was the one to experience the wrath of my teacher, even though I was the victim. That incident of being falsely blamed and punished for something I did not start, while the one responsible went unpunished, ticked me off. I was determined to take charge and be more vocal in defending my right to be heard. My determination was most likely a product of my emotions in trying to overcome the suppression I felt after being molested. I had to stand up for myself.

Another year passed and first grade seemed to go smoothly. My mom began to suspect that something was wrong when my second-grade teacher, Sister Cecilia, caught me in class with my hands in my pants touching myself. You cannot imagine how strange I felt at 7 years old having sensations "down there" and being questioned about something that felt good and didn't seem wrong. I did not know if this was normal childhood exploration or a replication of what my body experienced when being molested, but I was made to feel guilty for doing it. Whatever conversation transpired during the school's meeting with my parents made me feel like I was being blamed for doing something wrong. I did not understand. The question kept popping up in my head, "Did I do something wrong?" I think I must have been too young for any kind of lecture because I do not recall anything ever being brought up about the incident again. I remember feeling guilty and never did it again, I felt dirty at such a young age.

Every now and then, I find myself thinking of that innocent time in my life that really should have been innocent but was marred by events beyond my control. It also makes me think about how long these kinds of incidents have been going on everywhere to so many innocent children. It is so sad.

To produce a quality product, some ingredients should be left OUT.

???
??????????????????

What were some ingredients added to your adolescent years that

have helped you become who you are today?

Were there any ingredients that could have been LEFT OUT?

Were you or someone you know a victim of childhood

molestation?

"For I know the plans I have for you" declares the Lord
"plans to prosper you and not to harm you, plans to give you
hope and a future" Jeremiah 29

Chapter 2

MEASURING THE INGREDIENTS

"Good things take time for their miraculous manifestation."

Lailah Gifty Akita

Every good baker knows the importance of level measuring. Improper measurements can result in an imperfect product. Learning the skill of measuring, as in life, helps to determine what works best and gives one hope for the outcome of an awesome product.

THIRD OF A CUP

When I transitioned to third grade, I had a great teacher, Sister Mary Catherine. She was amazing, beautiful, and full of life. Her skin looked velvety, and her face housed big brown eyes that looked into the depths of your soul much like when a baby stares into your eyes. Her long, silky, chestnut-colored hair was exposed because that year the Catholic Church relaxed the rule of nuns having to wear a habit, unlike in previous years where they were covered from head to toe in all black except for their face. I felt more comfortable with Sister Mary Catherine because she looked to me more like a regular woman. She was a teacher who motivated me and recognized my talent, especially in music class. Sister Mary Catherine loved to sing and so did I. Since my mother now kept me attached to her like a second skin, she would take me to church for her choir rehearsals. I did not mind singing along in the choir because I learned how to sing all the songs in harmony, which is challenging unless you have a good ear.

My training allowed me to out-sing my classmates and become the lead singer in the school Christmas play. Singing was the angel sitting on one of my shoulders, but the devil was on the other, as I was still running into trouble at school. I felt like I was a square peg in a round hole.

My Catholic School education, aside from Sister Mary Catherine, was not the best. The rituals and beliefs clashed with my free-wheeling spirit. Wednesday was confession day, which as an 8-year-old, I did not fully understand what that meant. I followed the expected ritual of going into the box structure, kneeling, reciting some words, and telling the man behind the screen the things they expected me to say. Like: I was a bad girl for lying and cheating; I stole from others; I was disrespectful and talked back to my mother. I "confessed" to things I DID NOT DO! I hated when they made me go up to the railing, kneel, and say 25 Hail Marys practically falling asleep, since I remember hitting my head a few times. Because I did none of the things I confessed to, I decided to tell my teacher that I would no longer participate in this stupid ritual. This act of defiance resulted in my mother and me being called to Ms. Helton's office.

Ms. Helton, our principal, was the terror of our school. A stern, six-foot-two, wrinkled faced, shorthaired, hard, manly-looking woman with dark thick glasses, could have been mistaken for a priest in looks and in her voice. She never wore dresses or skirts and never smiled. I think her name was Ms. Hell and she changed it to work at a Catholic school.

Arriving at her office, we were ordered to sit down. I was then told I had to go to confession every Wednesday whether I liked it or not. In my now polished defiant attitude and tone, I said to Father, I mean, Ms. Helton, "If I have sins to report, which I don't, I ain't talking to no middleman. If I want to talk with God or confess something, I will talk directly to Him." I knew even then as a young girl that I had an intimate, spiritual connection with God, a relationship that has grown stronger over the years. God was listening because I ALMOST got expelled from school. I had to promise my mother and the principal that I would attend confession no matter what. Later, I told Mom I would make up lies about whatever I felt like just to do what Ms. Hell—oops—Ms. Helton, wanted. It is ironic that rather than instilling in me the virtuous qualities of truth and honesty, I learned how to manipulate and be deceitful. To stay out of trouble the remainder of the school year, I went along to get along. I could not wait to go to the 4th grade.

My hope for any parents reading this, if you have had a similar experience or have a child going through it, please ensure the moral principles he or she is being taught align with your beliefs. I understand the importance of discipline and having religious beliefs, but I don't think that a child at such a young age understands what they are confessing, especially if he or she is a good kid.

FOURTH OF A CUP

I have wonderful memories of Miss Williams, the craziest, most fun of all my teachers. She was the first African American teacher I ever met. We did not know any African American,

26

Chinese, Spanish, or Indian grownups—being only familiar with our own white, middle-class neighborhood. I guess you could say we were isolated from the real world. Miss Williams was beautiful, classy, sexy, and dressed like a model. She was not well received amongst the nuns and lay teachers because she was so modern. All the students loved Miss Williams, despite how she challenged us with hard work, made sure we did our homework, and assigned difficult projects. She was so down-to-earth. For some reason, the boys really liked her, especially the older boys, probably because she was sexy and built "like a brick house." Unknown to her, Miss Williams was blocking my game because at this age, I started really looking at boys, getting crushes, and feeling that puppy love. I was not serious about any one boy but did have a few crushes that were reciprocated. We would pass notes saying, "I like you; do you like me?" "Check YES or NO." Acceptance and friendships were major issues, particularly at that age. To belong is a basic human need, being a part of a play group, family, choir, church, or a community organization satisfies this need.

Today, for some, Facebook seems to satisfy their need to belong, which can be fleeting and unreal, leading to disappointment and emptiness.

Fourth grade opened the door to a variety of more pleasant home and school experiences, including good times spent with my mother in the kitchen cooking and baking. She would call me when I was outside playing with my friends. I would pout or talk under my breath about having to leave what I wanted to do most and go cook but Fridays were the exception; mom's day to bake fresh bread and our favorite cake or pie. I would stand by my mom's side watching her add a pinch of this or a spoonful of that, teaching me the skill of measuring just the right amount of ingredients for a cake. In time, I became the baker for our family, always getting rave reviews about how my cake was the best as each moist, rich slice after slice was devoured. On Fridays, the kitchen seemed to take on a cozy warmth enhanced by the soothing aroma of spices;it became my comfort zone. My zone was always interrupted when my brother and sister would run in and start a tug-of-war to see which one would get the bowl or the spoon after the cake batter was in the oven filling the house with a heavenly aroma.

These are some cherished memories. In-spite of what life's journey may drop at our feet, hopefully we will remember the special times. It was during those Mommy-and-me times that I developed my initial love of baking. Watching the wet and dry ingredients go in together, then rise, and the end product come out perfectly was my joy.

ADDING FLAVORS

At 10 years old, Mom enrolled me in the 4-H Club. 4-H represented four personal areas: **H** the **head**, **H** the **heart**, **H** the **hands**, and H for **health**. The organization's mission is "engaging youth to reach their fullest potential while advancing the field of youth development." I had to pledge my **Head** for clearer thinking; my **Heart** to greater loyalty; my **Hands** to larger service; and my **Health** to better living for my club, my community, my country, and my world. Quite a contrast from confession and Hail Mary's, you think?

The 4H Club experience grounded me. Year-round club activities allowed me to develop leadership skills, my passion for baking, and to enjoy the interaction with kids of different backgrounds. March, April, and May were the months when we prepared for various state fair competitions within our group and at the county level. Club rules allowed members reaching a certain age to go to a week-long camp during the summer. My friends and I were super excited about going, which meant school would end and we could pack our favorite things for the getaway. We laughed about how scared we were of snakes and ticks and speculated about what new things we would learn. This was my first experience with getting away from home and going by myself for a whole week to a strange location with strangers. Negative thoughts of being harmed by strangers or the precautions parents and kids focus on today were not prevalent back then.

There was trust in the organization and staff responsible for children during camp season. Sleepover camp was always an adventure away from the common dwellings of my neighborhood.

I remember the long bus ride departing from our school, full of kids between the ages of 10 and 15. We sang crazy songs like "99 Bottles of Milk on the Wall," "The Wheels on the Bus Go Round and Round," and any other song we could think of until we finally arrived at the campground. It was like entering another world. To this day, I still do not know the location.

There was a huge lake; lots of green grass covering rolling hills dotted with patches of picnic tables; a long, brown building beside two long green buildings. It was so pretty everywhere I looked. I had no idea where I was, only that I was in the woods, and not scared at all.

In single file, the girls were led to one of the green buildings, which turned out to be our sleeping quarters. We were told to pick out one of the bunk beds that lined each side of the huge room with high ceilings. The showers had no doors or curtains, so I guess that meant we would all shower together in one big room. This was my first time seeing other girls naked and my first time showering with a group. Fortunately, the toilet area had old wooden doors on each stall, but some girls would stand on the toilet and peep over into the next stall as part of the goofy stuff we did. There were about 40 girls in our building, which meant we had to share a few sinks and mirrors to brush our teeth and hair. The bunk bed had only one pillow, a thin mattress and sheets, and no blanket since it was summer. There were no closets to hang our clothes in, so we lived out of our duffel bags for six days.

We were taken on a short tour of the camp, which included the building where meals would be served. Our chores were to clean up after ourselves and on assigned days, each of us would have KP, (Kitchen Patrol), duties.

Wondering where all the boys were, we were told that they would be in the other green building. Each group had a counselor who, along with camp staff, were housed in another building. Counselors would take turns staying overnight in the girls' and boys' dorms to make sure no one was doing anything crazy.

Our group of girls was assigned the most gorgeous male camp counselor in the world, yes, Mr. Fine himself. His name was Bradley C. Davis, one name I will *nevvvvver* forget! I think I had the first, big crush of my life on this young guy who was trying to supervise and maneuver around the campsite with a broken leg. With a cast and one crutch, he was determined to be rugged and tough, doing by himself whatever was required of him. I managed to become a pest, trying so hard to help him that I know I got on his last nerve. I was just trying to be near him as much as possible. Bradley was always kind and professional, never getting mad or nasty toward me.

The groups at camp were named after Native American tribes, my group being named the Mighty Oneida Tribe.

We would sing our tribal song, chanting it day after day. I especially enjoyed the activities like archery, hiking, swimming, horseback riding, and racing games. All were new experiences and I loved to participate in each one.

Interacting with all the kids from different cultures, I learned that my father was so wrong about African American people. He always made negative comments and said things that he saw or heard from like-minded people where he worked. I found that the African Americans I was in contact with daily were not "bad" or different as he had described them to be. It angered me because they were NO different; they liked the same food I did, wore the same type of clothes, and got up and showered and brushed their teeth the same way I did. Unlike what my dad spewed about this group of people, I saw and felt there was no difference between us. Engaging in activities with children of different nationalities who did everything the same way I did was the most valuable lesson I learned. I also met my first black girlfriends, 10-year-old twins, which turned out to be a cherished memory.

It was so cute how we became friends. As I approached the building where I would be housed, these twin girls were sitting at the top of the steps. One of them asked me if I wanted a Hershey Kiss. I assumed she meant the candy, so of course I answered yes and ran up the steps to get some sweets. The twins huddled around me, one on each side and the next thing I knew, they puckered up and planted a kiss on my cheeks. "Surprise!" they shouted and the three of us laughed when they told me they had just given me a Hershey Kiss. I became enchanted with them, my new-found friends. My eyes and heart were opened to understand that there was a much bigger world out there that I was ignorant of, which included the wonderful world of spiders and snakes.

STIR TOGETHER

Still hyped up about camp after arriving back home, I was sitting at the dinner table telling my mom and dad about all the fun I had, all the different people I met, and about my new and exciting experiences. I also talked about Bradley, which must have been in a way that my father thought he was more to me than a camp counselor. Dad was furious, and mom's comments sounded like she thought I was having sex with him. For God's sake, I was only 10 years old! I assured my mother I was not, at that age, having sex with anyone. Now, as an adult, after confirming the molestation, I understood why they reacted the way they did during that conversation.

Back home in my neighborhood, I continued to hone my skills by participating in baking competitions. I would always win first prize for my Cinnamon Bundt Cake. I also raised money from the sale of raffle tickets to win, you guessed it, my Bundt cake. I would bake one cake and then go door to door in my neighborhood and sell tickets, one for a quarter and five for a dollar. The neighbors loved my cakes and usually would give up a dollar, which was a lot back then. At the end of the day, I would have my sister pull a winner from the hat and then take the cake to that family. They were always happy to win. Usually, I would accrue about 25 dollars for each cake from the sale of tickets; again, big bucks for one cake back then.

The fund-raising event, which served a two-fold purpose, would raise money for families in need and I was responsible for doing all the counting — stirring into the mix some math and management ingredients for the future baker, banker, and entrepreneur!

Every summer, we also went to a day camp located in the basement of a local church. I learned to crochet, make pot holders (old school craft), mold objects from clay, and play games like Monopoly. Summer activities were my favorite because I loved being outdoors in the sun. During the winter months, we baked, sewed, and bowled, which I loved. Because of my passion for bowling and the skills my gym teacher taught me, I became a Duckpin Champion at age 11 and I can still bust some pins. The ingredients of winning, giving, teaching, and creating filled me with a sense of accomplishment. To this day, I love being productive and accomplish more in one day than most people do in a week.

???

Did you experience puppy love?

Did you have a favorite childhood memory that you cherish?

Did you become involved with clubs or groups as a child that

you think benefited you as an adult?

"And the streets of the city shall be full of boys and girls playing in its streets." Zechariah 8:5

Chapter 3

GENTLY FOLD IN

"Life is pleasant, death is peaceful; it's the transition that's troublesome."

Isaac Asimov

I had two friends named Linda P. and Linda B, friends since 2nd grade, who by today's terms would be considered the "nerdy" type. One had long, dark-brown hair and glasses and the other had short, light-brown hair and an angelic face. Back then, we did not consider anyone a nerd, just someone who did not fit into the cool kids' group because they lived by their parents' rules and expectations…always good. Our friends gave us nicknames that we hated, especially mine. Everyone, except for the Lindas, called me Roach. Truth be told, I was going through my ugly duckling stage, and I was not cute. I had lots of fuzzy hair, braces, and real thick glasses.Eventually, Linda P. and I grew apart. Linda B. and I became closer. Linda B. was diagnosed at the age of 9 with Leukemia. During that time, about 1969, science and medicine was still learning about this disease and how to treat it, especially in children. Linda B. had such a sweet, friendly, truthful demeanor. Her mother, father, two sisters, and brother were just as awesome. I was always invited to sleep over; the highlight of the evening would be to sit on the floor and play school. We loved taking turns being the teacher.

I enjoyed these sleepovers, which were much different than the darker experiences at Mr.George's and Donna's house. This friendship with Linda and her family gave me a new perspective on love and family.

BREAKING EGGS

Linda's leukemia progressed, affecting her health and appearance. Over the next 2 years, I spent more time at Linda's to keep her company since she was missing more school. The times she was able to attend, the kids would make fun of her, saying she looked like a boy since she was losing her hair. When I visited her, she would sometimes hide from me so I would not see how much she had lost, leaving little for her mother to cover the bald areas. Linda became weaker as the weeks passed, she was in and out of the hospital and eventually her mother withdrew her from school totally. Hospital stays became longer and longer. Linda always kept in touch with me, writing letters to say how much she missed me, hoping that I was doing okay, always thinking about others. To this day, I still have those letters.

My mom let me spend the night at Linda's house when, at age 12, she was at a critical stage in her struggle with the illness. I really did not understand Leukemia and when I asked my mom what it was, her answer was that Linda had a "blood disease." Not knowing anything more about this disease, I still had unanswered questions like, "How do you get it? Can I catch it?" She never got around to answering those questions.

One day, after spending the night at Lindas, I went to the bathroom when I got home. I totally freaked out when I saw blood in my underwear. Crying and screaming, I ran downstairs to the basement where mom was doing laundry. "WHAT?" she asked, looking confused. I showed her my underwear while screaming hysterically, "I have the blood disease, I have the blood disease!!!!!"

I flung myself on the floor terrified, thinking I had the same thing Linda had. My mother was laughing so hard she fell to the floor into the laundry she was folding, tears running down her face and barely able to breathe. I was oblivious to hearing anything consoling. I stood there with swollen red eyes, upset, and growing increasingly angry that she thought it was so damn funny. Mom stopped laughing long enough to catch her breath and tell me not to worry, explaining what I saw was the beginning of my menstrual cycle

I was relieved but felt stupid. I realized I should have paid more attention during the "five-minute" sex talks she tried to have with me. At 12 years old, that day, I became a woman!

Unfortunately, while in the hospital, Linda B died a few months later. I never had a chance to visit her again, to say goodbye, hug her, or tell her how much I cared. I was crushed, a child not prepared to handle the hole in my heart from the loss of my best friend. Linda saw and accepted me for who I was; she was an important part of my life. There was no closure and even now when I reminisce about our bond, I get emotional. I was told the family held a closed casket, private memorial at church rather than at a funeral home. I'm sure it was very hard for them to bury their first-born child.

PICKING UP THE PIECES

Over the next few years, I intermittently kept in touch with Linda's mother and sisters, eventually each of us going our separate ways. Thanks to Facebook, we reconnected, excited to get caught up on the past four decades of our lives. Mrs. B. thanked me for the memorial garden that someone told her I created for Linda at the elementary school she and I attended. Knowing nothing about the garden, which was not my brainchild, I visited the school.

There in the garden, nestled between the memorial stones of two boys who had also died from our class, was a beautifully painted stone plaque with Linda's name on it. Being at the school and standing in the garden overwhelmed my heart with memories of our times together and the secrets we shared. During my visit, I felt a strong need to do something to create a lasting memory of our friendship. I contacted the principal to inquire about starting a garden club to ensure year-round attention and care of the site. I was informed by a teacher that students already tended to it as a school project to help them learn the process of seeding and growing plants. "It's a small world,"rang true when the teacher and I realized that she was the same teacher that Linda and I had over 40 years ago. It was her last year before retiring.

Our reminiscing somehow brought us to a discussion about cakes and the comfort I get from baking, which is when I offered to donate several cakes to the annual fall festival and made a monetary donation to the garden club to purchase more plants and tools. The students loved my cakes and later sent photos of the garden in full bloom. This warmed my heart and was appreciated by Linda's mother (to whom I had sent photos), who thanked me for giving added life to her daughter's memory.

Perhaps the students enjoyed meeting someone who had attended their school 40 years earlier; however, for me, it was strange walking the hallways again. I felt so huge in a tiny hallway. My brief stroll down memory lane put me in touch with childhood friendships, some of my favorite memories, recess, and boy crushes. But once again, the shadowy memories of the dark side of my childhood eased into my thoughts. I wondered how many children had experienced what I had, unsure how to tell anyone of the acts forced upon them.

As I exited the building, I prayed hard for those children to feel safe enough to tell someone and get help. I reached my car, got in, and shed some tears.

???

Did you have a nickname when you were young? Did it fit you?

Have you ever lost a friend or close relative when you

were a child?

How did you feel?

Have you ever gone back to your elementary school?

"He heals the brokenhearted and binds up their wounds" Psalms 147

CHAPTER 4
LUMPS IN THE BATTER

"Strong women don't play victim, don't make themselves look pitiful, and don't pointfingers. They stand and they deal." Mandy Hale

By the time I was 13, Mom went back to work full time and Dad worked all day and then would go to the golf lodge to hang out. My brother, sister, and I were home alone after school every day. We were assigned chores to keep us busy after doing our homework. I was put in charge of starting dinner and making sure the kitchen was clean. Our parents made it clear that no one was allowed in the house and to never have any boys visit. Well, my brother, who was a little older, thought he was in charge of everything and could do anything he wanted. Because his chores were to put out the trash, cut grass, and rake leaves, he would sometimes have his guy friends over to help, which meant that afterwards they would come in for a snack. A good cook, I could rattle those pots and pans and fix quick snacks that everyone enjoyed, with the added dessert of catching a glimpse of my slender but voluptuous body. My brother's friends liked what I cooked *and* how I looked!

My brother, who was a year-and-a-half older, was a sophomore at the local Catholic high school. My sister, who was a year-and-a-half younger, was just starting to notice guys and "hot momma" me was pretty much connecting with what seemed like every guy in the neighborhood. I'm sure we were just demonstrating normal teenager behavior, doing everything and anything we could get away with. Mom tried her best to be father, mother, and disciplinarian, but soon it became too much to handle. A lot of things happened in that house that should have never happened during those years. If I were to divulge them, there would be some hell to pay for all of us kids.

Mothers: make sure you keep a very close eye on your daughters, never leave them alone, especially during the tween ages and whenever boys are around. The hormones are raging and things WILL happen.

BEAT IT

My dad reminded me of Archie Bunker, opinionated, biased, and racist about every culture, religion, race, age group, and women. He worked as a repairman for the telephone company every day and golfed on weekends and after work. He was brought up in a military family and was a strict disciplinarian like his dad. I remember how I would sneak out to hang with my brother and his friends who drank and smoked weed on the street corner. During the warmer months, we would run the streets and forget what time we needed to be home — resulting in a date with Dad's belt.

Dad had his own way of getting our attention, which he did

not hesitate to use as often as he could. It was a special sounding whistle that emanated in the pit of his stomach, traveled up through his lungs, into his throat, and out his lips. The tone of it was worse than a shrill scream.

When my brother and I were out past our time, Dad would send out his ear-crippling whistle; we knew instantly we were in trouble. For Dad to whistle meant a butt whooping for me (never for my brother) with a heavy leather belt, one that left me with bloody legs and whelps. I would run up the steps getting whipped the whole way screaming and hollering, but it didn't matter, he never let up. I would often cry myself to sleep telling myself that Dad would love me someday, not understanding that this discipline was his form of love. My dad and I were never close like some fathers and daughters. Our relationship was more like that of a big brother type, giving me hugs like a brother would when I longed to cuddle up with him and hear words of reassurance and encouragement. I just wanted, at that time in my life to feel safe and loved, I needed that strength.

Fathers: The best thing you can do for your child (especially the girls) is to make them feel safe and loved. You must be their protector, their knight in shining armor always, this will keep them from falling victim to a weak man who may hurt them or take advantage of them.

This will also help them choose the right kind of person to have children with as well .Discipline is fine but equal measurements of love and assurance should be folded in.

The home scene worsened during my early teen years, causing me to think about leaving home sooner than later, as some teenagers do. To compensate for the lack of attention and affection at home, and the frustration of being caught in the middle of my parents' squabbles, I started to become flirtatious with a few older boys in the neighborhood. Mom tried to be more affectionate, but also felt neglected and unloved and started to spend more adult time with the man who made her feel valued, and it was not my dad...DUN.. DUN...DUN.

This was a very unstable time in my life, I had a sense of losing what I had been used to for so long. My father golfed his life away and worked all the time and my mother worked and tried to keep us together but was also trying to see her man-friend. My sister was still very young and in school and I was running around with anyone who would give me attention. The one solid thing I thought we had, even though it seemed dysfunctional at times, was our family. I could see and feel it falling apart quickly.

KEEP STIRRING

Even though the home scene was rough, I landed my first volunteer job at age 12. It helped me get out of the house and I learned a lot. Ms. Mary, a church friend of my mother who owned and operated a catering business, hired me as a server. I was impressed and inspired by the women who assisted her and their attitudes that were different from those I was accustomed to in my neighborhood. In 1974, these strong, independent businesswomen were instrumental in adding ingredients to my spirit for hopes of one day owning my own catering business.

Cooking, serving, and cleaning did not seem like work to me, after learning the basics, it became second nature. My catering work lasted until I was 16, with intermittent small jobs during the same time such as babysitting, waitressing, and clerical work. I also enjoyed teen activities like bowling, skating, and swimming. I got my learner's permit at age 16 and was hired for my first real job at the mall in the town center. Months later, I had the freedom to drive myself to and from work until I had my first accident in the mall parking lot. I stressed out, crying, and worrying about not being able to keep my license and paying for the damage.

Fortunately, the accident was quickly resolved, insurance kicked in, and life went on. I was learning about handling life's little tragedies at such a young age. The new job consisted of making pizzas, ice cream cones, sundaes, and selling hot dogs. My boss, Mr. Ed, taught me everything I needed to know and encouraged me, saying I was very responsible and a fast learner. I truly enjoyed the job and the new people I was meeting.

I believe my looks, height, and maturity attracted the boys in the mall and I did not discourage the attention. Later in my life, I came to understand that true beauty comes from within. You don't have to go around strutting your stuff—the right man will find you attractive just as you are. I wish I would have saved myself for marriage instead of giving myself away to so many LOSERS!!. I'm sure my self-esteem was low and I was still looking for love or what I thought was love in all the wrong places. It was too late. It's best to think these things out before you do them, as once the deed is done, you cannot re do it.

ONE BIG LUMP

One day at the job, I was approached by a guy named Mike, a red haired, freckled-faced, cheerful guy with a beautiful smile who worked in the store next to the pizza shop. He was a 21-year-old college student with his own car. I was taken in by his pretty green eyes and sweet gentle smile and said yes when he asked me for a date. Mike thought I was older because of my maturity, shape, and height. Our first date was innocent enough: walking through the mall, eating at a restaurant, talking, and getting to know one another. He was shocked to find out that I was only 16, younger than his youngest sister. We dated exclusively for six months, him acting like I was the best thing since ice cream. His parents and siblings loved me; however, the longer we dated, the less his mother seemed to like me. Perhaps she was becoming concerned about all the time we spent together or was looking for things she disliked. She was very suspicious of us — always wanting to know where we were going, for how long, and with whom.

Mike would yell at her to leave us alone and stop being so nosy. She made him feel like a child. He was embarrassed. I could not tell if Mike was a virgin because he acted very cocky and worldly. I discovered this when we were alone in his bedroom, and I made my move. Laying on his bed, we started kissing, it started getting hot, and the clothes came off. I climbed on top of his lean, strong body and as we did "the nasty," he seemed to enjoy the response of our bodies but suddenly wanted to stop. I jumped off him and asked what was wrong, and he said

he was a virgin and didn't want his first time to be like this, but it

was too late. We sat and talked for a few minutes afterward,

realizing that the damage was done. I think the truth was that he

was upset to find out that I was NOT a virgin. He must have

thought I was. I never gave him any indication that I was and he

never asked. I truly think it messed with his mind, I felt like he

really wanted to have a virgin girlfriend and be married before sex

but again, too late. After several more encounters, he was hooked,

wanting it all the time.

One night, we drove down Sunset Lane, a street near his

parents' house, and started kissing in the back seat of his dad's

Impala, steaming up the windows. In the middle of trying to get it

on, there was a knock on the window. A cop with a bright

flashlight shined it into the back seat right in my face. Because

Mike's dad was a cop, he was embarrassed. He got up from the

seat, zipped up his pants, and pleaded not to be arrested, thinking

his father would find out. He told the officer he was not raping me, when suddenly his tone became angry. It seemed the cop was shining his light directly on me, checking me out. I hurriedly dressed, feeling ashamed, embarrassed, and scared to death. Finally, the officer let us go and pulled off. We sat there for a few more minutes, shaking, and holding each other, saying we would never do that again, then we drove to Dunkin' Donuts to get some hot tea and calm down. Something about the human body and its internal warning system lets us know when there is a need for concern. It seemed like almost immediately that night I knew something was wrong. I told Mike, right then and there, that something physically was not right. My intuition proved me right. I later missed two menstrual cycles, followed by a urine test, which was proof positive for pregnancy.

Oh My Goodness, pregnant at 16, unmarried, and faced with having to tell my parents. I expected their reaction would be extreme; however, my greater concern was the worry I had about the new life inside me and what would happen next. Could I finish school, or would I have to drop out? Confused and scared, I cried for two weeks straight. I will never forget the night I sat in the middle of my bedroom floor and counted pennies from my piggy bank to roll because I wanted to make sure I would have enough money saved for my baby. I did not want my parents to have to pay for my irresponsible behavior. Little did I know that they had health insurance for me that covered expenses. I was too young to know anything about insurance or the amount of money needed for the birth. Another life lesson learned. My parents were furious and Mike's were disappointed with him for not using a condom.

While our families worked through the shock of their children about to become parents, I continued to work at the pizza shop and continued in school. Once the Catholic School administrators found out I was pregnant, as expected, I was told that I could only stay in school if I **DID NOT** marry Mike. This seemed backwards to me and made no sense at all. I was trying to do the right thing by getting married, only to hear that as a married student I could not attend that school. This was ridiculous and I was furious, so I left and enrolled into the local high school, where I excelled.

My mother did not want me to get married. Her thought was that I either keep the baby and stay single or put it up for adoption. There was no thought given to having an abortion, as it was a risky, often deadly experience for the mother as well as the fetus. Mom constantly heard me say how much I loved Mike, that I wanted to marry him, and keep our baby. So, she called a meeting with Mike and his parents to discuss our future. Everyone was quiet at first. I don't really think Mike's parents liked my parents, acting as if they were better than us. My mom took charge and the meeting ended with them agreeing that I would have the baby, my parents' insurance would cover costs, and I would finish school at night. Mike would continue college and we both would keep working, eventually get married, and begin living together to raise the baby.

In January of 1977, we got married. We did the best we could to prepare for our special day; he rented a tux, and I bought a second-hand wedding dress.

My mother took care of the flowers and cake and her friend Miss Mary made the party trays and drinks. There were about 85 people in attendance, mostly family, friends, and neighbors. My maid of honor was my soon-to-be sister-in-law and the best man was one of Mike's long-time friends. We had to get married in a Lutheran church because the Catholic church that my parents had poured all their hard-earned money into for all those years wouldn't do it. The Lutheran church was quaint and warm on that rainy cold day, and the reception was held in the basement. I had to add a pinch of humility and a pinch of fakeness to my face to hide the blush of being a pregnant child bride. Another statistic besides molested, bullied, and beaten.

In hindsight, I wish I had never married and just remained an unwed mother, took care of my baby alone, finished high school, and gone to college. I would have never had to endure the arduous turn my life took by marrying at age 16.

My loyal friends helped with babysitting and homework. My parents gradually adjusted to becoming grandparents but Mike's parents who still had young children at home did not look forward to taking on the role.

WHIP TILL SMOOTH

Mike's uncle owned a bungalow in the hills of Virginia, which is where we went for our anticipated honeymoon of two weeks. The day after our wedding, we drove to Virginia where we had a fun time: singing, talking, walking mountain paths, and enjoying each other's company. I was three months into the pregnancy, not really showing yet when into our second week there, a horrendous blizzard was forecasted to come through the mountains, cutting our honeymoon short. With this news, we gathered our stuff quickly and tried to beat the storm. Mike was determined to drive down the mountain side to the main road so that we could make it back home before the roads got too bad. Nature not only changed our travel but also changed us as a newly married couple. Unfortunately, the snow started falling earlier than we expected. It was coming down hard and fast. Unfamiliar with driving in blizzard-like conditions, our car slid sideways right into a ditch. We exited the car and after trying to push it out to no avail, we started walking in search of nearby homes for refuge, looking for anyone who might be able to take us in. My hands and toes were freezing. The chalets were spread out, dotting the mountain. I will never forget the feeling of despair, hoping we could find anyone to help us and hopefully find someone who was eventually going anywhere near Baltimore.

As we were walking, a haggard-looking woman in a raggedy van pulled up and asked if we needed help and where we were headed. We told her what happened and that we were hoping to get back to Baltimore. Only by God's grace, she said that is where she and her family lived and offered us to spend the night with them in their cabin before heading back in the morning. We gladly accepted, grabbed our stuff out of the car, and hopped into her van. It was a night I will never forget, a honeymoon story made for TV, straight out of The Addams Family, including a mentally challenged Uncle Fester living up stairs.

His sister, our host, warned us that he was on medication and that he mostly stayed in his room, just in case we heard noises. We were told not to speak to him if we did see him wandering around the house. My husband and I, scared with thoughts of what he might do to us,finally fell asleep on their L-shaped sofa. The way we held each other, with our arms extended above our heads with hands clasped, allowed us to feel somewhat safe.

During the night, 'Uncle Fester' emerged from his room and walked past us into the kitchen, scaring the crap out of us. Our arms, numb from trying to sleep in that crazy position, felt like they had been chopped off. Being so entangled in each other and unable to get up from the sofa, we looked at each other thinking this might be our last time together in "death-amony." We broke out laughing hysterically until we were crying, while at the same time we were trying to be quiet. What did we get ourselves into?

We did not know these people; they could kill us and eat

us for breakfast. Did we make a mistake by taking her up on her

offer to spend the night?

Then we heard Uncle Fester returning from the kitchen and we

pretended to be asleep. Uncle Fester disappeared, leaving us afraid

to go upstairs to the bathroom which we both desperately needed to

use. Clinging to each other, we tip-toed up the stairs, down the

hallway, and stood outside the bathroom door. As our luck would

have it, Uncle Fester was in the bathroom, so we bounded down the

stairs faster than two hungry dogs chasing a bone.

We laughed over and over about our situation and finally used

the restroom after we heard him come out. Needless to say, we

didn't get much sleep the rest of the night. Morning came and the

whole family greeted us in the kitchen for a hearty breakfast. They

talked about leaving Mike's car and coming back to get it the

following week. They seemed very nice but we couldn't wait to get

back home. Of course, the ride back seemed to take forever.

Contrary to memories newlywed couples usually have of fun-filled

days and passionate nights, we laughed for months afterward about our Addams Family Honeymoon. Even though it was early in our relationship, the humor of our adventure camouflaged signs of Mike's controlling personality, which I mistook for his need to protect me. I have learned it is often a red flag of control issues when a guy shows too much "protecting me" behavior.

There are real gentlemen out there who will protect you and NOT try to control your every move. *Pay attention to all the signs, if you don't FEEL right, then it's probably not right for you. Whatever you do, don't ignore your gut instincts. If the batter is lumpy, it's not right yet. Test the batter and whip out the lumps over and over till you are sure it is right for you.*

???

What are some of your fondest or funniest first job memories?

Have you ever dated or met a spouse on the job?

Do you have any wild honeymoon stories?

"God causes everything to work together for the good of those who love Him." Romans 8:28

Chapter 5

SPREADING THE BATTER

"In life, things can always go wrong, so always keep your heart strong, carry on and never give up hope."
Mouloud Benzadi

We lived in a small room at my parents' house, me with my big pregnant belly and Mike with all his books. The baby was due in July, so I stopped working and finished my senior year at night school, graduating with straight A's. When I transferred to night school, I was so advanced I graduated a half year early, beating the odds of becoming another statistic, a high school dropout. Because of finishing in night school, I missed activities like the senior prom, the annual Senior Week in Ocean City, and all the fun parties. The greatest disappointment was not being able to take the triumphant walk along with my original class to receive my diploma.

GREASING THE PANS

In the last few weeks of my pregnancy, I helped Mike through his last weeks of college, writing and typing papers, quizzing him before exams and a myriad of other tasks associated with graduating. Despite his leaning on me for support, most of the time he seemed annoyed with me and the pregnancy, acting as though he was ashamed of me and the baby; or perhaps it was his big ego telling him he was superior to us. The fact that he and my father hated each other and his mother's escalating demonstration of dislike for me increased his discontent.

Our beautiful, healthy daughter Lexi arrived during the summer of 1977, weighing in at 7pounds. The doctor said she was the most beautiful baby he ever delivered. Of course, he probably told every new mother that, but she truly was gorgeous. From the moment I saw her tiny face, fingers, and toes, the color of her eyes and the shape of her lips, she became my world. The same was not true for Mike; he disliked the attention I paid to Lexi. Jealous of the time I gave to her, he became verbally and emotionally abusive, pushing me around, calling me names, mocking me, yelling "You don't know what you're doing. You are no kind of mother. You're a dummy." However, he never helped either.

A few months later, Mike and I were discussing something that escalated when I did not agree with him. Unhappy with me, he swung his arm and slapped me across the face so hard I fell backwards into the sofa. Three rooms away, my father must have heard his hand connect with my face. Dad burst into the room, punched Mike in his face, knocking him to the floor and told him to NEVER put his hands on me again. Mike got up, dazed, got his coat, and rolled out the front door without a word. I was hysterical and in shock from both encounters as I watched my husband leave the house in anger and Dad, who seldom showed his emotions. I felt my whole world had ended.

Dad told me if I went back to Mike, the baby and I would have to leave his house. Confused by my emotions and not knowing what to do, I decided I had to stay with my husband. I caught up with him at his best friend's house, where he went to unwind. He saw me and ran to me asking for forgiveness and I just started crying. He told me he didn't mean to hurt me, and I believed him, although I should not have. Adding to his rage was the turmoil Mike experienced with his parents. His mother, at every turn, was inventing ways to start trouble between us, so we talked about it and decided to rent an apartment of our own a few miles away. Things seemed to go well for a few months.

Initially, I did not work after Lexi was born; however, when she turned 6 months old, I landed a job as a waitress at a local restaurant. Because of all the catering experience I had, I picked up waitressing fast and I was good at it. Ms. Betty, my hostess, loved me and assigned me many tables that brought great tips. I made about 100 dollars a night just in tips, which was REAL good money back then, in fact, I earned more than Mike despite his having a college degree and working two jobs. Unfortunately, my earning power threatened his ego and before long he began verbally abusing me, accusing me of prostituting myself. OMG, I was barely 18 years old, I was trying to be a money-making, responsible member of the family. Evidently, he didn't see it that way. I quit my job and endured the verbal and mental abuse just to keep him off my back. A couple weeks later, I found another job with a better hourly rate but no tips. Mike seemed to be okay with this new job, which was right around the corner, I guess so he could drop in and keep an eye on me at any given time. I was working at a catering hall, a grueling 60- to 70-hour work week, on my feet the whole time. Now, instead of being angered by my earning more than him, my paycheck never seemed to be enough for "His Highness."

I had to leave Lexi with babysitters, mainly his mother, who I secretly hated, knowing, as I believed, she had control issues like her son. She was quite manipulative and condescending to me all the time. She totally acted as if she was Lexi's mother and treated me like I had no clue how to raise a child or even take care of one.

For almost two years, I worked hard to learn the catering business from the inside out. I became the head waitress after three months and managed several events all at the same time, running from hall to hall, keeping everyone in sync. My schedule and responsibilities kept me away from Lexi too much. I wanted to be with her to bond during the time when bonding is critical. When I was able to be with her, I was too exhausted to give her my best. Mike's mother acted as if she was helping to fill the void in my absence; however, I saw right through her manipulative acts. The grueling hours took its toll on my body, and Mike's mother became increasingly hard to deal with. Even he had issues with her every day and could see her trying to control things. I kept telling him we needed to move and get our own place far away from her and finally his job offered him a position that would help facilitate that move. I put in my two weeks' notice and started looking in the paper for a house. I was very happy to finally quit that job.

POUR IT OUT

We were blessed to find a small ranch-style house near the beach about 30 miles away from his mother. It was a shotgun rancher with chipped white paint, blue shutters, and a small backyard. As soon as I saw it, I fell in love. The location was great, and we could walk to the beach, which was a few blocks away. I knew I could do a lot of the work the house needed and would enjoy making it cute and homey. Because of needing work inside and out, we negotiated a great price and we were able to make the deposit right away and move forward with the paperwork.

Another life lesson learned early, buying a house and all the legal paperwork that goes with it. I was a 19-year-old homeowner.

Upon moving in, I painted the white cinder block exterior and huge wrap around porch a soft butter yellow, the shutters and trim a milk chocolate brown. On the porch leading to the yard, I hung plants and laid green indoor/outdoor rugs. Inside, I put up sconces and hung artwork to make it warm and inviting.

Lexi was two-and-a-half years old and excited about the move, especially her spacious pink "girly" room. She ran into the room with her arms wide open like she was trying to hug the air, then rolled around on the floor laughing and giggling. She was so happy. Living life as a teenage wife and mother was not easy or fun. Today's TV shows do not depict the reality of the experience back in the 70's and 80's. A teenager having a baby was like wearing a scarlet letter around your neck and being judged by the world. Despite having my daughter, I refused to give up, refused to escape into drugs or alcohol, and refused to live in despair. I believed that God would see me through as I was trying to *whip it up*!!

Settling in, at almost 20 years old, I was eager to begin earning a living outside the home. I quickly landed two part-time jobs nearby, one as a cashier during the day in a food service cafeteria with free daycare: the other part-time position at night as a restaurant hostess. My talents and good work ethic earned me a friendship with the bosses, and I was quickly promoted to key positions, making decent money.

It was then I began dreaming about launching my own small catering business. One of the managers at the restaurant allowed me, for a few hours a week, to start my business out of the kitchen. I managed to get some of the smaller jobs that the restaurant didn't really want and clients who could not afford the restaurant's prices, so I offered to do assorted catering trays for them. The word-of-mouth spread, and I soon had a nice stream of business coming in. This venture proved successful until Mike started to complain that I was spending too much time making money and not enough time taking care of him, his daughter, and the house. Again, to avoid mental and physical abuse, I let go of the business. To stay busy at home and make some side money, I started baking cakes again, cakes totally different from the 4H Bundt cakes.

The idea originated with my sister-in-law's fantastic recipe for a moist and delicious yellow cake. Her cake recipe was the bomb! It was interesting how this all came about. Vicky, my sister-in-law, had a daughter who was turning a year old. She had taken a class in cake decorating, wanting to make her daughter's first birthday cake special. The decoration was a clown with about 20 different colors of icing, totally star tipped (a decorating term for icing shaped like little lumpy stars). The cake looked awesome and tasted so delicious, it melted in my mouth.

Normally, I was the one in the family who did all the baking, this was my first experience eating HER cake. Vicky said this was her first and last attempt at decorating a cake. Some people steal recipes or try to copy the ingredients; I was about doing the right thing, so I asked Vicky if I could have the recipe. She said, "Sure, no problem! YOU CAN HAVE IT! I NEVER want to do this again." I thanked her, then as soon as I got back home, I started trying it out, folding in my own ingredients, making my own icing, and testing different flavorings. My first public taste test was the cake I served at Lexi's 3rd birthday party. Everyone raved about how good the cake was, with an unusual flavor much different than any other cake they had ever tasted. From then on, as Lexi grew, my cake-baking skills grew along with the demand for the cakes. I believed I had found my niche: I loved my new coworkers, my new neighbors, my new house, and this new recipe.

When I did not have to go to work, Lexi and I spent our days together doing mommy-daughter things: spending hours at the beach, then going home to clean the house and prepare dinner for Mike. Our routine worked for a while and was good until Mike would have a bad day or if he thought I had done nothing constructive all day (which to him was almost everyday.)

Mike would get "heated up" faster than the oven temperature I used to bake my cakes. Again, the abuse began and continued in spite of telling my mother and mother-in-law about the verbal name-calling and physical pushing. As a young woman with a kid, experiencing the only long-term relationship I ever had, I did not know what to do, besides reach out to them hoping they could help. In the 1970's there was not, if any, public conversation about the topic of spousal abuse; at least I was not aware of what resources were available. Mike's mother refused to acknowledge his behaviors; my mother was with her new husband since she and dad had divorced. I remember her telling me, "You made your bed, you have to lay in it," adding "You must be OK with the abuse because you are still with him." These words spurred me to try to get out, but to no avail. Where was I to go?

Nobody liked Mike, perhaps they felt he was struggling with a mental or emotional issue of some kind, but in reality, no one wanted to get involved. My neighbors, who had become friends and did not generally intrude in our life, finally told me I should leave him, after hearing him loudly berate me. How embarrassing.! I truly didn't know what to do, or who to turn to. I just knew I couldn't take much more. I felt like the control and the abuse was getting worse. I knew I was not a dummy, and I was responsible and could take care of myriad things all at the same time, but Mike thought differently. He continually put me down, told me how and when HE wanted things done. He would treat me like a dog, and rub my nose in it, whatever it was that bothered him. He was Mr. Perfect. Ha!

I remember we were at his friend's house, and he didn't like something I said, so he announced we were leaving and told me to get in the car, he started driving and threw my purse out the window, started calling me names and then stopped the car and told me to get out and walk all the way home.

I didn't even know what he was mad about. He was truly sick. Of course, I didn't get out. I screamed back at him and made him go get my purse. I threatened to tell all his friends and call the police and that's when he changed his tune. His big ego and reputation would be ruined. I think he knew I finally had enough.

Was this Love? Was this what a relationship is supposed to be? He would constantly project one face of the nice guy to our neighbors and his friends and then turn around and growl in my face about the least little thing that bothered him. I have heard this is called the Dr. Jekyll and Mr. Hyde syndrome. Some people call it bipolar because of the sudden mood swings. I just knew I was growing weary of trying to figure out who was going to show up each day and how to dodge any curve balls.

SCRAPING THE BOTTOM OF THE BOWL

One day after work, Lexi and I cleaned the house after which I cooked dinner and had it ready to serve piping hot when Mike arrived home from work. As I was setting plates on the table, the phone rang, it was his boss. It infuriated him to be getting a call at dinner time, no matter who was calling. Lexi was getting fussy after her long, tiring day; so, while Mike was on the phone, I gave her some peanuts to keep her quiet as I went about reheating his dinner. Mike hung up from his conversation and immediately flew into a rage. This transition of emotions was not new but this time he threw his dinner plate on the floor, moved toward me, and slammed me up against the kitchen wall. My confusion about what triggered the pendulum of his emotions was nothing new; however, I could not figure out this Dr. Jekyll, Mr. Hyde transition from merely being on a phone call. He said he was mad because I gave Lexi a couple of peanuts, which he felt would ruin her dinner. WHAT???

When I tried to explain, he picked me up with his hands tightly around my neck and threw his full body weight against mine to crush me up against the wall. With a distorted look on his face and in a state of violent, uncontrollable anger, he screamed, "I could kill you right now!!!"

OH MY GOD ... I could hardly breathe! My thought was to just get OUT, get away from him NOW!!!

Shocked, scared, and feeling cornered, my adrenalin kicked in, causing me to react by kicking him in the nuts hard and swift enough to catch him off guard and make him loosen his grip. Slightly loosened, I struggled to escape, dropped to the floor, got free and ran toward Lexi. Screaming that I was going to call the police, I snatched her up and ran across the street to my neighbor's house.

Embarrassed, I had no choice but to involve them. When the police arrived and questioned Mike, he was in his Mr. Hyde state, little Mr. Nice Guy. Hysterically, I showed them the marks around my neck and on my arms and asked for an escort into and out of the house to collect our clothes and personal items. If at no other time, this time I should have filed charges against him but not wanting to hurt him or his career (SILLY ME), did not. I remembered years earlier, my dad warned me that this would happen again in my relationship if I stayed with him.

He was wise and experienced enough to see through the façade. I was too naïve and hopeful that our marriage would work. I knew I had to leave and take my daughter, but I had nowhere to go. I swore to myself to never go back to him, and I NEVER did.

That night, I called my girlfriend Jane to ask if we could come there, then called another friend who drove us to Jane's house, where she graciously offered us a place to stay until I could find my own place. This arrangement worked for about two weeks, when she regretfully told me her baby's daddy was going to move in and I had to move out.

Move where? My first thought and action were to call my dad, who had remarried and bought a home that had an apartment in the basement. As it turned out, it was already rented to someone else, which basically left me homeless. WOW!! Another statistic! Homeless, with a child.

FACT: "Sixty percent of domestic violence victims are strangled at some point, during an abusive relationship.... Statistically we know now that once the hands are on the neck,

the very next step is homicide." *Sylvia Vella, clinician, and detective with the San Diego Police Department.* Reported by the *United Nations Office on Drugs and Crime (UNODC),* every day across the world, 137 women are killed by a partner or family member. It says it makes "the home the most likely place for a woman to be killed." More than half of the 87,000 women killed in 2017 were reported as dying at the hands of those closest to them." Additionally, *The World Health Organization* called domestic violence a global health problem of epidemic proportions, while the *United Nations Office on Drugs and Crime* cited that 50,000 women around the world were killed by partners or family members. In Oct. 2016, Act 111 was signed into United States law, making non-fatal strangulation a criminal offense.

???
????????????????????????

Have you ever been in an abusive relationship?

Did it ever come close to being fatal?

Do you know anyone with Dr. Jekyll / Mr. Hyde tendencies?

Have you ever had to make a split-second decision that would change your life and that of your child forever?

"Do not make friends with a hot-tempered man, do not associate with one easily angered or you may learn his ways and get yourself ensnared."
Proverbs 22:24-25

Chapter 6

THE HEAT IS ON

"The wounded recognize the wounded." Nora
Roberts

Never would I have imagined that Lexi and I would be
living in a car for three months. I had to think of a location where
I could easily get to work, find somewhere to eat, wash up, and
change clothes without anyone suspecting we were homeless.
Directly off the main route to my job at the cafeteria, there was a
side street with an isolated hill where we could park and sleep
without anyone seeing us and very few cars passing by. Lexi's
daycare was on the same campus as my job, so we would go to a

nearby McDonald's for breakfast, use the bathroom, brush our
teeth, freshen up, and change clothes. I would then drop her at the
daycare and go to work. She hated it when I dropped her off. She
would scream, "Don't leave me, don't leave me, come back!" It
was heart-wrenching because I had to work. I started to wonder if
someone might be hurting her or mistreating her while she was
there. I eventually questioned the staff, but they told me that all
the kids act like that. She never said anyone was hurting her, but I
still had my suspicions.

After work, I would pick her up and go to the new mall in town to use
its restroom and eat. We walked for hours to kill time. Lexi loved it. She
got to run and play until she was ready to drop from exhaustion. We would
head back to the isolation of the hill and hunker down for the night. I would
recline the front seats as far back as they would go and put pillows between
them so that we could snuggle close. To take the focus off our situation, we
would talk about things that made us laugh, mostly silly kid stuff, until she
fell asleep. Gazing up at the stars most nights, I would pray for an answer as
to where we would go next and think about possible resources or people
who might be able help us, hoping and praying God was listening.

I tried to be happy, easy-going, and positive all day, even though I knew what awaited me at the end of my shift. NO ONE knew what I was going through. I was too embarrassed and ashamed to tell my mom, or dad, even when he told me the basement apartment was taken; no one in my family knew of my situation. I often wondered why they never really tried to contact me during this time but I guess they thought everything was hunky dory since they didn't hear from me. The old saying, "No news is good news," isn't always the case, but I would never have told them even if they would have asked. I was blessed to at least have a job and a car, so I was not looking for shelter or begging on the street corner.

I saw homeless people every day; never did I think I would be one. Most people think the homeless are drug or alcohol addicts, but everyone has a story as to what brought them there. I will long remember my feelings of shame and hopelessness combined with desperation. There I was, crying myself to sleep again.

The bible tells us that weeping may endure for the night, but joy comes in the morning. I had to trust and believe in that verse many times. I have never looked at homeless people the same since and I always try to help them whenever I can without judging them. Who knows where I would be right now if it weren't for some kind people who helped me and for the Grace of God?

There was an African American guy named Larry who worked with me. He wanted to date me and from time to time would ask me out. I told him I was married but had recently left my husband because of the abuse. Larry seemed to care about my situation and used humor to lift my spirits. We talked a lot, which allowed me to let down my guard and I shared with him that my daughter and I were living out of my car. Becoming even more concerned for our safety, he told me that his mother had space in her basement where we could stay. Larry was surprised and thought it was crazy that I had so many relatives and none would help.

Me, "Little Miss Independent," explained that I did not ask for their help because I was embarrassed, ashamed, and felt like a failure who had hit rock bottom. Larry arranged for me to meet his mom, Ms. Kathy, who showed me her basement located in the ranch-style home where she, her husband, and four sons lived. She said she knew it wasn't much, but it would be better than living in a car.

She was very sweet and caring. Her husband and boys didn't help her much, she always had to stay on their tails about everything. She invited me to get my stuff and move in whenever I felt comfortable. A day later, we moved into the basement, where my dank spot had a box spring and mattress on the floor with no sheets, cobwebs, and a flimsy blanket. The green painted cinder block basement included the laundry room, storage space, and an oil drum located near the furnace that wreaked an unhealthy, nauseating smell I will never forget. I went to Goodwill and got some sheets and blankets to make it more comfy. This cold, dimly lit damp space served as temporary housing and was tolerable for a short time.

Ms. Kathy often heard me praying to God for help and invited me to go to church with her. I accepted the invitation, not realizing I would be the only white girl in the congregation. It did not matter, as I was welcomed with open arms. Before long, I joined the choir and enjoyed singing God's praises, reminiscent of the times I went to rehearsal with my mother and being the

lead vocalist at school. Lexi also loved attending church, making friends with kids, and traveling to other churches when our choir performed. Like me, it gave her a feeling of being connected to a loving family, grounded in something other than our unsettling circumstances. Meanwhile, I saved all the money I could and steadily looked for an apartment and a better job with benefits.

I was in a bad place in my life — homeless with a kid and concerned about how I was going to provide for us. I caved in and asked my mom for financial help to get back on my feet. She told me her new husband would not allow her to give me cash unless I sold her my jewelry as collateral, so I sold her my diamond engagement ring for $200. I needed the cash to put toward a deposit on an apartment. I never got the ring back; nor did I care to, however, Mom saved it and gave it to Lexi on her 21st birthday many years later, which made it very special.

Praise God! He answered my prayers. I landed a new job and Lexi and I moved out of the basement and into our own sparsely furnished apartment. We were too far away to keep in touch with Larry, Ms. Kathy, and the choir members. This was before pagers, cell phones, and Zoom, although we did visit every now and then. Most of our furnishings were donated by friends or from Goodwill. Lexi liked the new neighborhood and her new room. It was a lower middle-class area, with lots of kids her age, mostly girls. She made friends quickly. After paying the security deposit and first month's rent, I had no money, certainly no savings, but I would soon be starting my new job. I did what I could to make some cash on the side baking cookies, cakes, and brownies and selling them to the new neighbors. My new job had great hours, pay, and benefits and was only about 5 miles away.

There was also a daycare right across the street that most of the employees used, so it was perfect. I gave my old cafeteria job two weeks' notice and prepared myself for the new job. I was so excited!!

LEVEL THE BATTER

Trusting that Mike would be cooperative, I permitted and arranged for him to have visitation with Lexi. My life AGAIN quickly changed after he KIDNAPPED her!! Give me a break!!!! On the day this happened, I had dropped her off at his house with the agreed upon plan that I would return in six hours to pick her up. When I returned, however, Lexi was not there. Instead, I found a note from Mike saying that I would not see her anymore and that he was going to file for full custody because he thought I was dating black men. The truth was, I knew a lot of black men, but I was not dating *anyone* because we were still legally married. I knew better than to fall into that trap.

When Mike took Lexi, he kept her from me for 4 months. Every day, I tried to find out where she was. I called neighbors, friends, and relatives and finally the police; none of them would help, the police said Lexi was not gone long enough to consider her missing. I could not work or think straight, worrying constantly where she was, who she was with, and what might be happening to her. I didn't trust him or his friends. It was horrible not knowing where she was, much less the fact that I knew she missed me as we were so close. I had nightmares of her screaming and crying out for me. I would go looking for her every chance I got, banging on the doors of his relatives' houses until someone helped me. I found out that she was staying at his grandmother's row house in the city. I never thought he would leave her with his grandmother and an uncle, both of whom were not capable of keeping up with a 4-year-old. I drove to the house, pounded on the doors and windows until someone called the police.

I knew my daughter was inside and I was desperate to take her home with me where she belonged.

Mike's grandmother finally opened the door after the police arrived. She told them I needed to talk with Mike, who was not at her house. She phoned him and he said he would come, but never showed up. I cried and pleaded with the police and his grandmother, but I was not allowed to take her with me. Lexi was screaming and crying at the window, like in my dreams, wanting to be with me; they would not let her. I could hear her screaming, "Mommy, Mommy don't leave me, don't leave me!" The pain in my heart was unbearable when I had to walk away and turn my back on her, knowing she was watching me while she was begging me to take her. All I could do was cry and keep walking as my heart ripped out of my chest. A few days later, I found out that they had moved her to his sister's house about an hour and a half away close to the state line. I was afraid they may take her to the bungalow in the hills across state lines, which would make it harder for me to fight for custody. I had to do something right away.

Initially I was angry, crushed, and felt helpless. I cried out to God and screamed, "Please Help Me!!!" At that time mothers did not have many legal rights since fathers earned more money and were usually the total source of income for the family. I realized being frustrated and angry was not going to resolve my situation. I was determined to raise hell until someone heard my side and I got action. I called the non-emergency police to see what I could do. After hearing my concerns and knowing that he may go across state lines, they told me to immediately go see the Court Commissioner who was on duty 24 hours a day. *Yay! Just what I needed, Thank You, Jesus!* I went to the Court Commissioner to tell him what happened and requested an emergency custody hearing. GRANTED!!! The papers were typed up and ready to serve. I also filed for an immediate non-contested divorce while I was at it. Why not get it done all at once?

Mr. Mike, "The Man," must have thought he was ahead of the game, that he was smarter,being a college graduate and all. Much to Mike's surprise, after the commissioner heard my plea, the sheriff served him the papers and ordered him to return Lexi to me immediately; an official court date was to follow.

OHHHH... he was FURIOUS!!! Of course, he and his family retained an attorney who then subpoenaed all my records. When I reviewed the documents sent to me by his lawyer, I whited out my name, filled Mike's name in and sent the papers right back to him to subpoena all his records. HA HA HA!!!

When we appeared in court, I brought a box full of receipts as evidence of all the money I spent and the costs of everything I had been providing for Lexi. There were also receipts showing the cost of related expenses for me to flee from Mike, his abuse, and find a safe place to live. All my journaling of events proved helpful to the court case. Mike had nothing to support his claim that he should have full custody. Not one receipt. It was a long battle and several meetings with The Division of Child Support before they finally ruled that the divorce was final and that we would have joint custody. I fought to split the week right down the middle, hour for hour. Mike would have Lexi during the week, Monday night to Friday morning and I would have her from Friday afternoon until Monday morning.

After the last hearing, Mike's lawyer pulled me aside to tell me his client was a jerk and that he would never represent him again in any matter. He also said that for me to white out the names and add Mike's in on the subpoena was a stroke of genius, something he had never seen in all his years of law. Ha!

By this time, Lexi was almost 5 and going into kindergarten. The joint custody decision turned out to work well for me because I could continue to work my full-time job and take on another part-time job. Mike, who was to keep her during the week, instead left her with his mother while he worked his "one" job and romanced a bunch of women. Mike hardly ever spent time with Lexi. Basically, his mother was raising her. As much as I tried to protect Lexi throughout her childhood, her attitude and actions showed she was scarred from the inconsistent parenting and turmoil within the family who tried to turn her against me.

She was confused by what they spewed about me and would often ask me what certain words meant. I told her not to worry about what they said and just enjoy our time together.

Fast Forward: When Lexi was 13 years old, Mike remarried and bought a home about an hour away. He wanted Lexi to live with him and his new wife. I supposed he envisioned the three of them living as a perfect little family. He did not expect her to turn against him and refuse his offer. Remembering how good she had it at his mother's house, no way was she going to live with him, her new stepmother, his rules, and stepbrothers.

Of course, Mike accused me of influencing her decision and was surprised to hear that I knew nothing of it. She knew she wanted no part of him or his life with his new family. Lexi ended up staying with her grandmother during the weekdays and remained with me on weekends. Throughout the years, she would visit her father but never moved in.

AIR BUBBLES

Meanwhile, during all the hell that was breaking loose, I had started my new day job at the large cafeteria, and I loved it right away. The people were pleasant and helpful to work with,which made it fun and took my mind off the drama in my life for a little while.

When I started with the company, I was the dishwasher for eight hours a day. The dishwasher is the most important job in any food establishment, because without clean dishes, pots, pans, and utensils, no one can do anything. The three compartment sinks were piled high with pots and pans waiting for me every morning. Guess what? I loved every minute of it, as I passed the time meditating, singing, whistling, and building some muscle. I was a fast learner, soaking in as much as I could and was moved around to different positions to be flexible on the schedule.

Promotions came quickly, from pot washer to server, server to cashier, cashier to delivery driver, and finally to manager. My boss, whom I loved for his commitment to mentoring me, recognized how easily I learned the business and often complimented me on how responsible I was. Driving the company truck, delivering food to other buildings, and handling cash receipts prepared me for my next promotion. After two years, I became the satellite manager, traveling to three facilities, managing the vending, all the money, and all of the personnel.

I was picking up shifts at night here and there, waitressing, bartending, and catering, as well as doing cakes, which kept me busy and money coming in so that I had no time for men. By the Grace of God, things seemed to be progressing smoothly.

I loved my weekends off, spending them with Lexi and the neighborhood girls. We often had sleepovers and almost every weekend during the summer we would take trips to the beach. I taught all the neighborhood kids how to swim, skate, bowl, ride bikes, ride horses, count money, practice their manners, respect, and how to pray. Going to the movies followed by roller skating in the parking lot was my favorite thing to do. I was a young adult living vicariously through the lives of Lexi and her friends. I could feel they enjoyed being with me, evident today by how some continue to stay in touch and call me mom. I was very protective of the children because I personally knew the dangers of pedophiles. I would always talk to their parents first and make it a point to get to know them so that they would trust me with their child.

I gave full transparency when it came to my life. I was given their permission to take their children with me and treat them like my own. I was strict but loving, I had rules, but I let them be children. I knew to keep them close to me and to each other and always kept my eyes on them.

BIG BUBBLE

There was an elderly, retired Army general and his wife of many years who lived across the court from us. They seemed like a normal sweet old couple. The neighbors and I later found out that he was molesting some of the girls in the area; fortunately, none of those in my care. One of the kids who told on him said she knew of another girl he molested. After observing his behavior, I found him to be creepy and suspicious. He would stand on his apartment balcony, call to the girls playing outside to come over then drop candy down to them. I was told by one of the older girls that when they asked for more candy, he would tell them to come inside his apartment then have them lay down on his bed next to each other. These were innocent little girls who were just following his direction in hopes of getting more candy. They may not have expected or understood what happened to them next, but I did. I don't know to this day what transpired in that room but after I anonymously placed a call to the police and reported what I suspected they did their own investigation. About a week later, he was arrested and charged as a pedophile and according to the newspaper would spend the rest of his life in jail. Evidently, the abuse was worse than what I suspected.

Years later, old neighbors told me he died while incarcerated and his wife moved away to live with family. I was glad he was no longer a threat; however, it caused me to wonder how many children or young women under his command while in the Army were possibly molested by him. Even today, it is difficult for me to understand how pedophiles or sexual predators who are professionals such as teachers, doctors, and high-ranking servicemen throw away their careers, families, and lives because of their illegal sexual behaviors.

How could they let their sexual urges over rule all the years of hard work and sacrifice and when caught, lose it all for the sick pleasure of the moment? I still struggle to comprehend this.

When there are air bubbles in the mix, most of the time, we bang the pan on the table before putting it into the oven.

This helps to pop the bubbles so the cake will rise evenly and not have big gaping holes after it's baked. Just like in the batter, as in society, you must get the air bubbles (bad people) out or it could ruin the growing child.

STICK IT IN THE OVEN

All the things that happened in my life and around me made it very hard for me to trust men, but good things can happen when you least expect it, or so I thought. I was not "really" looking for a man to be in my life but at times thought it might be nice to go on a date. Leaving work one snowy day, I was trying to dig my car out of the parking lot when I met a man named David. He walked over to me and offered to help with my slow digging.

We quickly became friends and started what soon became a "we like each other" connection. David impressed me as being smart, helpful, and looked good at 5' 8", with a strong, thin body. He had big dark brown eyes, short hair, and the biggest pearly white smile on earth. It was time to let a man into my life, so we dated for two months without getting intimate — which was great for me but seemed kind of strange that he wasn't even trying. One night, he dropped by unexpectedly then dropped the bomb that he was in love with someone else. Well, that explained his behavior. WHAT? WHO? WHEN? Well of course later, I found out that he had been very close to marrying someone right before he met me. They split up and he found himself dating me, then changing his mind and going back to her. WOW!!! Of course, we stopped what never really blossomed into any kind of serious relationship and shortly thereafter he got married to the woman and had children. After David, I dated a few guys of various ages and races, some younger, some older, but none of them seemed to have anything special to bring to the table.

Several of the guys just ended up being long-time friends. Others I became intimate with couldn't seem to get themselves together either financially or just be monogamous. Too many times, I would catch them cheating and break up with them. I would immediately dismiss them and forget about the whole relationship — totally wipe it off my heart and head for good. I would hear them begging and pleading that they would never do it again and that they wanted me back, but I never believed it.

Lil' Miss Independent was back and on a roll. I was not putting up with no dumb stuff. I'd rather be by myself than deal with any more crap. Most mothers will tell their daughters, "You can do bad all by yourself. You don't need someone else dragging you down."That is the truth, it just took me a while to get it. Your mother has been through things, please listen to her.

Okay, Girls, listen up! Do not ever believe that line about never cheating again. If you catch him cheating BEFORE you get married, then thank him for not wasting any more of your time, kick him out, or just leave and never look back.

If you catch him AFTER you have tied the knot, you can get a good lawyer and take him for everything he owns and make his life miserable or just walk out, but don't believe his lies, don't stay with him, and don't give him any more chances!!! Once a cheater, always a cheater.

??

Have you ever been homeless or know anyone that has

been or still is?

Do you know anyone who was kidnapped by their parents?

Do you agree once a cheater always a cheater or can a zebra change his stripes?

Rejoice in our confident hope, be patient in trouble and keep on praying." Romans 12

CHAPTER 7

BAKE IT TILL YOU MAKE IT

"Feeling lost, crazy, and desperate belongs to a good life as much as optimism, certainty, and reason."

Alain de Botton

I was 25 years old and AGAIN on my own, despite disappointments. I was working hard, staying in shape, and saving money, basically having to fake it and hoping I would make it. I was still loving life, but I needed to get a new "How to Find a Good Man Meter" because the last few readings were whack.

Meanwhile, to pick up the slack of not dating or having a man in my life, I continued to pick up part-time night jobs. At the day job, my boss recognized my management performance and offered me my own cafeteria to run. He took me under his wing, and I owe much of my success to his mentoring.

The thought of managing my own cafeteria both thrilled and scared me but I accepted the challenge. The schedule for the new position dictated I leave home at 4:30 a.m. for the 30-mile drive. I supervised one employee, an older woman, who was quiet but helpful. My new boss, the regional manager, a friendly petite woman, periodically stopped by to teach me how to run the business. We offered a continental-type breakfast menu, with a switch to lunch in the afternoon, offering deli meats and salads. My workday ended at 2:30 p.m., which allowed me time to exercise before the start of the second job. With full days and nights, working from 4:30a.m. to sometimes midnight, I was exhausted, but no matter how tired I was during the week, my weekends belonged to Lexi and her friends.

I still have photos of all the kids, lined up in a row on the floor in their sleeping bags when they would spend the night at my apartment. I was so proud of those kids. Over the years, all the children I took care of finished their schooling, achieved good grades; some attended college while others married and had families. Not one of them ever got into trouble, went to jail, or engaged in any type of substance abuse; all became productive citizens. Like baking a cake, you must measure the right ingredients into children's lives to get a good product.

Fall and winter weekends with them often called out my inner baker, resulting in the aroma of cake and brownies filling the apartment especially during the holidays. We would hold bake sales, helping to perfect my skills and help the kids to make money, which I would match and then take them shopping for Christmas presents for their parents. For about 7 years, I never bought anyone Christmas or birthday gifts, since I was in survival mode. Instead, I would bake cakes and cookies and give them as gifts. Every year, I would look up new recipes in cookbooks, which are rarely used now due to Google, and try two or three new ones. I taught myself how to decorate cakes without today's nifty tools seen in You Tube videos. I had to rely on cookbooks and the old-fashioned method of trial and error. Of course, eating the mistakes was our favorite part. YUMMY!!

I would bake off dozens and dozens of cookies and brownies, go to the grocery store, and get the styrofoam trays that they used in the meat department, which were just the right size for a couple dozen goodies to fit on. Lexi and I would lay them out across the living and dining room areas, fill them with cookies, wrap them in saran tightly, then put bows and name tags on them. We would box them up and put them in my trunk to be delivered throughout the holidays to all my friends and neighbors. They loved the treats but after several years, my work hours went into overtime and the cookie trays came to a halt. My friends and neighbors were not happy, and I felt bad but the only free time I had, I wanted to spend with Lexi.

At work, I was learning how to run a food service operation and it boosted my confidence in managing. I learned about payroll, inventory, food costs, cash handling and bank deposits, as well as contracts and forecasting budgets. Eventually, I launched another small catering company using that cafeteria, making creative party trays. The cafeteria continued to grow under my management to where I can proudly say we added three more employees. One of those employees remains one of my best friends to this day. I also gained some new catering business from the offices within the building. The people loved the fact that we offered this feature, and they would not have to order out and pay higher prices plus delivery. They used us for all their office parties and meetings and my manager loved the increased sales.

Since everything seemed to be going well at the cafeteria, with more hours being spent there, I decided instead of driving back and forth all week to a second job, I would seek out part-time opportunities after work closer to the cafeteria. Fortunately, I connected with a divorced father with two young boys who needed a maid. I never thought of doing the job of a maid, but I knew I had plenty of experience with children and cooking, so I figured it would just be another addition to my resume. After meeting the family, I felt it would work out great. The dad always seemed totally exhausted after working all day and needed me to help with the chores. He paid well for a few hours of work each day.

I would pick the kids up at school right after I finished the cafeteria job, take them home, clean the house, fix their lunches, cook dinner, and make sure they completed their homework. Their dad was usually fast asleep on the sofa the whole time I was there most days. I treated his kids like they were my own, demanding certain respect and discipline, which they were not used to. Some situations were funny, and some were not, that's when I would wake the dad up and get him on it. They knew they were in trouble then and I would laugh all the way home.

After a few years of working for the man, he met and married the lady who lived across the street, they became a combined family, and no longer needed my services.

She had three kids and a mom who lived there, and he had the two boys. It was truly a Brady Bunch Family experience. I knew I would miss the kids, but they were growing up and able to take care of themselves by then. After a little break, I took a new night job as a waitress at the Airport Hotel only two nights a week so that it would not be so exhausting. I also met the man who would eventually become my second husband. By now, I felt I was "seasoned" from past relationships, and at this point I was so done with men. I had no interest in dating. But wouldn't you know on my first night of work, I got the cook's attention. The head waitress took me on a tour of the kitchen where Ronny, the cook behind the counter, pointed at me and said, "There's my future wife, right there!" I guess for him it was love at first sight. He was Chef Ron; I was a 28-year-old waitress with an 11-year-old daughter not wanting any relationship. Rejecting many of Ronny's requests for a date, I was ready to start a new chapter in my life, ALL BY MYSELF!!!

WATCHING IT RISE

During the first few months of working there, I was continually sexually harassed by a male employee. Sean, a tall thin black man in his early 30s was respectfully friendly when I first met him, but within a day or two, he must have thought he had the right to do what he wanted to me. He was not shy nor slick about it. Sean reminded me of the old men in the neighborhood when I was growing up who would come close, as if to whisper in my ear but instead stick their tongue in it. He would grab my butt as I walked away and tap it every time, he got close to me. He would quickly lick my cheek whenever he could get close to my face. I would slap him, push him, and tell him to leave me alone EVERY time. Not taking my warnings seriously, I took my complaint to management, who did nothing. My next move was to go to upper management with a threat to sue the hotel if they did not fire or transfer him. Management still did nothing, which made things worse. I was about to quit, when one day Ronny saw Sean touch me inappropriately and as I screamed at Sean, Ronny flew into a rage, physically attacking Sean telling him to never come near me again. Ronny was twice the size of Sean and normally soft spoken, but not that day.

After that incident, Sean was MIA (Missing in Action) — GONE! — and I didn't care.

This experience caused me to see Ronny in a different light, believing he cared for me and wanted to protect me. I felt violated by Sean and ignored by management, who interpreted his actions as playful and innocent. INNOCENT MY ASS!! If I would have given him any smidgen of an inch, he would have taken a mile or two, and ... HE WAS MARRIED. I should have told his wife! What a piece of crap !. Looking back, it seems nothing was offensive; unlike today, just about everything is offensive. We must be careful of what we say, who we say it to, and *how* we say it. Thankfully the "Me Too" movement again has brought sexual misconduct into the light and is swiftly holding offenders accountable.

Gently, Ronny persisted in asking me for a date and after a while, he wore me down. After he broke through the ice around my heart, we began spending a lot of time together. After work we would meet at my house and walk and talk for hours. He would make sure I was in and safe, then leave. Eventually, he started staying overnight and got to meet Lexi, who took to him quickly. Eight months later, Ronny proposed. I believed he genuinely loved me. I knew I had found my "happily ever after" and I said YES!

I worked at the Airport Hotel for a year when my hectic schedule caught up with me. I was exhausted and kept falling asleep while driving to and from both jobs. God must have known I needed to rest because He had a plan. It was three days before Christmas when the airport got slammed with downed flights due to a severe snow storm. I had locked up the cafeteria for winter break and had just made it home in time before the roads got too thick with snow. Ronny was already home cooking dinner. He was off that night, and we had planned on giving our gifts to each other at dinner since we knew we would probably be working the rest of the week.

The airport got hit with a blizzard, Ronny and I both got hit with the flu. We couldn't go anywhere.

It was horrible being sick together; neither of us could move or get out of bed for 10 days. We thought we were going to die, get fired, or both since it was the worst time to be away from our jobs with the onslaught of guests staying at the hotel. Since we were critical staff, timing was bad; no cook, no waitress — we were doomed. Our coworkers thought we had gotten married and gone out of the country on a honeymoon. Landlines were down and there were no cell phones back then, so we had no way to tell them where we were and how close we were to death. Ronny went back to work as soon as he could, but not me. My employees ran the cafeteria for another week without me until I got better. It was the worst sickness I have ever had in 60 years.

LOOKING SCRUMPTIOUS

It was the second week in January before I returned to work, still not fully recovered. I made the decision to quit my night job at the hotel. Months later in May, Lexi and I met Ronny after he got off work and went to the courthouse to tie the knot. He put on a nice shirt and pants in the car and I had on a simple shirt and skirt. Lexi was in her play clothes but cute enough to be our witness. After the simple ceremony, we went out to dinner to celebrate our nuptials and our new family. We lived in my apartment for a few months when, during our conversations, I started planting some seeds about buying a house. On this idea we did not agree because he was taking care of his mother and felt a house would be too much responsibility. We were both making good money and had little debt, when all the sudden his car died. Ronny needed to get reliable transportation, so he went and bought a new car. Not one to give up, while looking into our credit scores, I finally persuaded him to consider owning a home. We wanted to find something we could grow in and close to both of our jobs.

First, we looked at townhouses, but I wasn't feeling all the steps and especially if we were going to have kids, I didn't want to be climbing steps at 75 or 80 years old. We continued looking and found a modular tri-level house under construction in a new housing development that was conveniently located. We went into the model, loved it, picked out the plot, filled out all the paperwork, and put our deposit down right away. We knew we had found the perfect home. Together, we enjoyed shopping for paint, furniture, chandeliers, and other décor, even though it was delayed gratification since everything was put on lay-away until the house was completed. The plan was that when the house was ready to move into, all our purchases would be paid off and delivered. This gave us time to go in and paint without having furniture and rugs in the way.

Just like my first house, I did most of the work myself. Ronny could work those pots and pans, but I was the one who could work the drill, saw, hammer, and nails.

I painted, put up wallpaper, chair rail, crown moldings, mirrors, and pictures. Everything matched and was ready for the finishing touches to be delivered. Two days before the deliveries, Lexi and I got some blankets and spent the night on the floor, all cuddled up on the new rugs, loving our new home, the smell of fresh paint and looking up at the sparkly star stick-ons that I adhered to the ceiling. This reminded me of our time in the car looking at the stars and I realized then just how far we had come, ONLY BY THE GRACE OF GOD. I prayed a prayer of gratitude and cried happy tears till I fell asleep.

The friction between me, my ex-husband Mike, and his family escalated when they found out I married a cook who happened to be a black man, bought a house, and moved further away. They tried to make my life hell, calling me all kinds of racist names in front of my daughter. As hurtful as it was, Lexi and I were able to talk about everything this time as she was older now, allowing me to answer her questions, telling her that in time she would understand the truth and see people for their true colors.

After totally moving in and getting settled, Ronny worked his full-time job and a part-time job with a caterer friend, making good money at both, along with the good salary I earned from the cafeteria. I was in the union, vested, and had excellent benefits. We were really in a sweet spot for the first time in a while. We were able to pay off all our debts, leaving only the mortgage and Ronny's car payment. One night, I became ill and could not sleep. I had a stabbing pain in my stomach, so I laid down thinking it may have been indigestion from some broccoli I had eaten.

After hours passed and the pain and feelings of nausea had not subsided, at my request, Ronny drove me to the emergency room, where I asked to be tested to see if it was my gall bladder, stomach, or possibly my appendix. This was a pain I had never felt before.

Diagnosis, I was pregnant, a surprise to both of us since I had not missed any periods. I could not tell whether Ronny was happy, blown away, or overwhelmed. He seemed to be down.

He had no energy and was laying around most of the time; he became defensive whenever I said anything; seemed hopeless and negative. I was uncertain as to why he was reacting as he did and I constantly assured him that everything was going to be alright. His responses told me he did not believe what I was saying. An unplanned pregnancy and thoughts of how the family will make it with another mouth to feed has been known to cause some insecure feelings and worry. I don't think Ronny fully realized that financially we were in good shape.

During that time, pregnant working women did not have the benefit of taking maternity leave but had to take a two week leave of absence, which is what I requested in order to keep my benefits and pay level. I continued working as long as I could without going into labor on the job. My employees and some of the people in the building at the cafeteria threw a baby shower for me. It had been almost 12 years since Lexi, so I had to start all over and many items that I received had been updated anyway. Ronny lost himself in his two jobs. He was unable to cope with the idea of having a baby and occasionally smoked marijuana to take his mind off things.

I had a very healthy pregnancy and gained a lot of weight. Our daughter Darcy was born on Labor Day 1989, pushing into the world after 28 long hours of labor. She weighed 10 lbs. 8 oz., was gorgeous, with a head full of dark hair against beautiful olive skin. Ronny was the happiest man alive and for months enjoyed the congratulations and well wishes from family and friends.

Life went well for a little, while but hanging out with the wrong people at the wrong time, his "little" marijuana habit started to affect his everyday life. I do not have concrete proof, but I believe one of his "smoking" friends started lacing the weed with cocaine.

First, it was just smoking marijuana, then marijuana laced with cocaine, which progressed to free basing by burning the cocaine on a spoon over fire. Ronny may not have been aware, but I understand drug dealers do this to recruit new users who continue to seek that initial "high"— eventually leading to addiction. Ronny was hooked!

He was what is known as a functioning addict. His boss,

coworkers, family, and friends had no clue he was using drugs,

that's why they call it functioning, but I could see much more

than they could.

POKE IT

I believed Ronny really loved me, in spite of how he was

damaging our family. It was a stressful balancing act, as I had to

go back to work. Luckily, my company placed me at a factory

cafeteria close to where we lived in a management position with

good pay. I hated giving up the cafeteria and all the friends I had

made, but knew it was best for me to be closer to home. I worked

the 3 p.m. to 11 p.m. shift and Ronny worked from 6 a.m. to 2

p.m. Our schedules allowed us to take care of Darcy and not need

to put her in daycare. This arrangement did not last long. Usually,

I could depend on Ronny for his help in caring for her; however,

my loving, responsible, goal-oriented husband and father

transformed into another person.

He would come home all hours of the day and night, freaking me out with unbelievable stories. He would read the Bible then sit and stare like he was on a journey to outer space, causing me to wonder if he would ever return. There was no smell when he was using, no evidence, except when he would stay in the bathroom too long, where I would find spoons and balls of tin foil. I had no choice but to finally call NARC-ANON to speak to someone to get information on what to do. My life became a different kind of crazy, different from my first marriage, where I experienced physical abuse. Why was I unable to choose a good man, one without abusive or addictive tendencies? Was it because of the abuse I experienced as a child that kept drawing me to men with their own history of abuse and insecurities? Was I grasping for any kind of love or physical affection? I should have sought out a therapist.

GIVE IT A MINUTE

The cafeteria position was a Godsend, however, the crew needed plenty of training. They gossiped about each other, lacked a good work ethic, and the cook COULD NOT cook! Most plant employees "brown bagged" their meals. Sales for the second shift were horrible because of their "sucky" attitudes. I became a woman on a mission to empower my staff, improve their cooking skills, and hopefully get the sales up.

I also established incentives, organized staff meetings, taught them how to cook and bake, then rewarded their hard work. The crew bonded and earned trophies, which I picked out and paid for. Within a few short weeks of giving samples of our new food items, we began doubling and tripling our sales; the plant employees LOVED the new food and employee attitudes. The two other shift managers became angry and jealous. They started hiding food so that we could not use it and complained to upper management, leading an anti-Diane crusade because our shift was doing noticeably better than theirs. They constantly whined about everything related to our success. The big bosses were getting too much pressure from the other two managers and decided to intervene.

After all my years and experience, I was OUT, let go. Unfortunately, I did not have the opportunity to appeal the decision or to present how my team's improved productivity had resulted in burgeoning sales. Somehow, it was in their heads that we were stealing. That did not make sense; clearly, our sales were way up and the product was gone. They "pink slipped" me anyway! They called it downsizing and eliminated my shift, but I knew what was up. I had been with the company a total of 12 years when they laid me off, resulting in a nice severance package of 12 weeks' full pay.

Everything happens for a reason is what people say. I was hallelujah happy for my pink slip vacation and never looked back or wanted to return to the company. This break gave me time to think of all the things I really wanted to do and stay home with Darcy. Circumstances that could have led to negative outcomes provided an opportunity for me to launch my first registered business, "Affairs of the Heart Bridal Consulting and Party Planning." I participated in bridal shows, researched vendors, kept logs, and set up appointments with clients from my little office in the basement. In the 80s, The American Bridal Consultants Association did not exist. I originated the idea of working freelance and getting paid a finder's fee from the vendors instead of charging the client for my services. I used my knowledge of cakes and catering experiences and parlayed it all to work to my advantage. Caterers who did not have their own pastry chef or cake decorators also provided me with a stream of new business. I enrolled in a public relations class that taught me how to get on TV, which I successfully did with an appearance on a local morning news show. Before I could get back home from the interview, I was bombarded with phone calls asking about my services. Eventually, Ronny also started cooking for some of the caterers. I thought he was trying to stay close and help with finances but later I found that he was using the extra income to support his habit.

As some people say, "All good things come to an end." Within a year, there came a surge of bridal consultants with new rules and mandatory certifications, much like operating a daycare center. This resulted in having to discontinue that part of my service and focus solely on cakes. Later, I was contacted by an old cafeteria manager and asked if I would like to take on a temporary position in a nearby cafe while its manager was on maternity leave. This cafeteria suffered from the same issues I addressed in my last position: low morale, poorly trained staff, thievery, and an uninviting work environment. All this was nothing new to me, even the one aspect of daily travel downtown to collect money and data from the satellite venues. The employees were stealing, which was difficult to prove and even harder to catch them; they were slick. I continued as temporary manager because it was a nice little chunk of money for 6 weeks' work, but as soon as the manager on leave returned, I left and was relieved to get away.

THE BATTER SUNK

Ronny's addiction to cocaine worsened. One day he would say he lost his wallet, the next day he would say he was in a car accident. This went on and on and on.

His unbelievable, imaginary events told me he was losing touch with reality, evidenced by him being fired from his job. I believe it became too much for his boss as well. Most days, Ronny sat around the house dazed, bored, and dejected. The last straw was when he came home supposedly from looking for a job and told me he had been robbed. Believing that this was another of his fabricated stories, I confronted him until he finally, for the first time, confessed that he was hooked and unable to function.

To hear it from him, confirmed the fears stirring inside me as to what this really meant to our relationship and our family. My next thought was how he was supporting his habit. Immediately, I checked our bank accounts and it felt like I had been punched in the gut. Our joint accounts had zero balances. Nada! Not only had Ronny plundered our checking and savings, but he also emptied my own personal savings account by getting my pin number after opening my mail. My husband, whom I loved and trusted, admitted to having a $100-a-day or more addiction. My stomach sank. I felt so sick.

I started crying hysterically and sucking in air feeling like I couldn't breathe, thinking I was about to lose everything — AGAIN!!! Then I ran up to my room, closed the door, sprawled across the bed, and prayed like never before. I could not believe that this man, whom I thought was my 'happily ever after," had sent me right back to survival mode. What was I going to do??? Days later, Ronny came home visibly shaken, sat down next to me, and sputtered out that one of his friends owed a kingpin money. He said he was visiting his friend when the dealer unexpectedly dropped by, put a gun to his head, and demanded that he pay his friend's debt. Was I to believe him or was he telling another one of his wild, questionable stories? Not knowing, I could not take any more chances with my life and Darcy's. At that moment, my husband of three-and-a-half years became a stranger to me. I could not even look at him anymore and realized that I really did not know him. I did not know his friends, how much he owed, and to whom. I did not know if this dealer would come after me and Darcy to collect or retaliate by rape or just outright kill us.

I DID know that I was done with the uncertainty and growing fear. I tried everything I knew to get him off the drugs, identifying resources for him to work through his addiction. I begged and pleaded with him to get help; he was defiant and in denial about his problem. He kept saying he could get off the drugs by himself.. I WAS DONE!! My world had collapsed and gone to hell. It was over! All I could do was pray at this point.

Note to anyone going through this: MOST addicts cannot get off of drugs by themselves, whatever you do, don't believe their stories, don't give them money, don't let them out of yoursight. Even when you think they are sleeping, lock up all valuables, keep their so-called friends away, and get them into rehab, a 12-step program, or church. Be there for them, but do not enable them. Sometimes it is best to let them hit rock bottom, so that they realize the only way out is up, and they have to want it badly enough; otherwise, it will be a futile attempt. Ronny still says twenty-five years after getting off the drugs that it is a daily battle not to go back on.

My instincts immediately made me start to think about how to remedy this. My first thought was to close all the bank accounts and change the locks…he had to GO! I knew I had no choice but to go back to work, I had to get money back in the bank accounts before the mortgage was due. The next day, I packed Ronny's clothing and belongings in large garbage bags and put them outside on the curb in front of our house with a note telling him not to come back. I then changed the locks on all the doors. As expected, when he pulled up, he saw the bags and the note, wanted to know what was happening and after trying to get in he begged and pleaded for another chance, but I could not risk our lives because of his drug habit. I really had no clue where he would go or who might let him in. My heart truly broke into pieces. I cried for days.

I knew I had to get myself together. I prayed for good babysitters and jobs to pop up so I could get back on my feet.

I worked as a part-time bartender for a few months, which helped short-term, but I knew I needed to find a steady job. I applied for a position as a teacher's aide, which resulted in a job as a substitute teacher assigned to a school down the street from my house. God is good! I vowed I would not lose my home because of someone else's irresponsibility.

Not financially able to pay the mortgage due to the drained bank accounts, I refinanced my house through HUD, for which I had to write many letters and submit what seemed like hundreds of documents seeking approval. HUD approved me and had a mortgage plan that lowered my monthly payment, easing the situation until I could find a better-paying job. I continued to substitute teach, bake cakes, and I also created and operated a before-and-after daycare in my home.

Being on my own again, I had to do whatever was necessary to make as much money as possible. Ronny was not sending any child support money and had, in fact, disappeared for a while.

I believe he moved in with his mom, eventually ending up in jail for non-payment of support. In jail, he was able to kick his drug habit and prepare himself to rejoin the work force once released.

Sometimes you have to fake it until you make it. I had to wear a smile all the time to hide the pain and the feeling of despair inside me. The heat was on, the oven was hot, the batter rose, then sunk, but by the Grace of God, I was able to salvage some scraps and make some cake pops. As for the rest of the cake, just like in life, some things you just have to dump and start over.

???

Have you ever lost a job, then started your own company?

Have you ever been harassed at work and been ignored by

management?

Do you know anyone on drugs or have you ever been an addict?

"Then they cried unto the LORD in their trouble, and He delivered them out of their distresses." Psalms 107:6

Chapter 8

Dump it and start over

"Sometime the hardest part isn't letting go but rather learning to start over." **Nicole Soban**

At 33 years old, I found myself starting over again. Lexi was almost 16 years old, and Darcy was almost four. Lexi, who was living with her boyfriend's mother, asked to move in with me, deciding that her situation there was becoming intolerable. When she moved in with me, her boyfriend came along, which was something I disapproved of right away; however, that did not last too long. Her boyfriend, a real low-life thief, brought frustration and chaos to our home. I had one tenant, a young college girl, renting an upstairs room to help with the mortgage. Lexi and the tenant's personalities clashed, along with finding out her boyfriend was stealing everything he could from everyone in the neighborhood while I was at work and Lexi was at school. One night when I refused to cook dinner for him after working long hours, I told him to fix his own food. He was so spoiled by his mother that he immediately decided momma's house was better and started bashing me about it; so, I took them back to his momma's house right away for good. Although I loved Lexi and wanted her to live with me, I didn't need all the drama in my life at that time. I was still trying to mend and heal myself. I didn't want what happened to me at 16 to happen to her. I believe within a month of being back with his mom, Lexi and her boyfriend broke up and she never dealt with him again. She had become the strong independent woman I knew she was, and I was proud of her.

After a few months of taking odd jobs, doing the daycare and teacher assistant jobs, I found a new steady daytime job as a restaurant hostess at one of the local hotels and I loved it. The position seemed perfect; it worked well with my daycare hours, the pay proved decent, and my work schedule allowed me time to go home, watch the kids after school, and bake cakes. It was basically a breakfast and lunch operation, someone else covered the dinner shift. Even though the money was coming in a little better now, it was still not enough to pay the mortgage and the bills that had accumulated during the time I was unemployed and had to use credit cards to pay for groceries and household items. I felt like I was in a lot of debt and would never be able to get ahead, truth was it really wasn't much. I sought out an attorney to file bankruptcy so I would not lose my car or house. She was very nice and told me that I should NOT do it because I only owed about 4,000 dollars; but at that point I could not see ever catching up. She took care of the case, only charging me for the paperwork and filing, for which I was very grateful. We went to court and within minutes I was relinquished of paying all the debts. Now I qualified for another statistic.

Bankrupt.

TRY A NEW RECIPE

For nearly 2 years during my bankruptcy status, I avoided getting into any man-focused relationships. The grief that accompanied the end of my marriage dampened my desire to be with someone else. I experienced bouts of depression and thoughts of how and why it always seemed that anything connected to a man never worked out for me at any level.

BAMMM! When I least expected it, along came a fine young buck: about 6 feet tall, gorgeous, and slim with the right amount of mocha. We crossed paths in the lobby of a catering hall where we were both attending the same wedding. Our eyes met and it felt like lightning hit me. He smiled a sweet smile and winked. WHEW! I tried to play it off, acting like I was not interested and kept on walking. I kept seeing him in the crowd throughout the night until the party ended. He came up behind me as I was leaving (scared me a little) and asked me if I would like to get a drink. I turned around slowly and asked him if he was old enough to drink; he laughed. He assured me he was legal (barely) and I said yes. We walked across the street to a local lounge and talked until the wee hours. He was fine, sweet, and funny; the only caveat was the age difference.

He was 22 and I was 35, a 13-year difference. I liked him despite knowing all he wanted to do was to "rock my world" (oh, you know what I mean!). And he most certainly did for about four months. He was, as they say, "All that and a bag of chips." Although he was a mama's boy, I found out he got into trouble with her for spending time with me. Even though he was legal, I believe because he was living under her roof, he had to go by her rules. Our "sexsationship" ended quickly when he almost got fired for showing up late for work one night. He told me he worked hard to get that job and could not afford to lose it. I understood; he was a bright light during a dark time, and I was grateful for the few months we had.

After 3 years of working as the hostess at the hotel, I had an argument with management and felt I was treated unfairly. I quit and took a day job right down the street with the competition; only this time I was waitressing, the same shift, making great money, leaving me time for cakes and Darcy. I decided to take a sabbatical from relationships, to stay single, and earn as much money as I could. I gave up on the before and after daycare around this time because Darcy was ready for full time day school. Since she was there all day, I kept my waitress job, took on a part-time ice cream shop job and still did part-time substitute teaching, as well as doing cakes. While I did substitute teaching, I also became active in the PTA, becoming treasurer and then president.

Even though things were flowing and going, I needed a steady job with benefits. I applied for a position at the local grocery store in the bakery hoping to be their cake decorator. They called me in for an interview and cake test right away. I felt like I did a pretty good job and so did they. I landed a part-time position with benefits and a good starting salary. My only concern was that I had to work the hours around Darcy's school hours because I could not afford daycare. The boss I had there was young, sweet, talented and very fast. She wanted things done quickly. That worked for me, I became very efficient, and trained in other areas of the store so that I could be used for more hours, eventually becoming full time. I had to give up the ice cream shop and substitute teaching to do it full time, but it was worth it. The money was good, the benefits were great, and I was finally able to pay all my bills and start saving for my future. Management would send me to five different stores to do all the cakes, learn new techniques and increase my speed. Sometimes I even took Darcy with me as she got older and she would help put flavor labels on the packages. Everything in my life seemed to be in divine order again. Thank You, Jesus! God had seen me through again.

I met some of the best people in my life during the 8 years and five locations I worked for the grocery store. One lady who would come in and ask decorating questions turned out to be one of my very best friends to this day. Some of the managers and employees keep in touch with me now. The few girls that were in the bakery with me when I first started, rudely called me "Fatty Patty," since my middle name is Patricia. I was 37 years old and about 70 pounds overweight. I didn't look or feel good. I knew I had to lose weight but working with cakes and sweets didn't help.

One young man named Donte, an employee in the produce department, and a senior in high school, showed his compassion for others when one of the women in the bakery, known for being mean spirited, began loudly teasing me about my size. Donte heard what was happening. He quickly and harshly yelled at the woman to leave me alone. She tried to bark back at him, but he quickly shushed her. I was touched by his caring actions. He had a good laugh when I told him I was going to adopt him, and he would be the son I never had. I don't think he realized that I was old enough to be his mother. From that point on, we developed a friendly, platonic relationship. We would talk sometimes when we worked the same shift, since the bakery and produce departments were right next to each other.

We continued to work together here and there until he went to college. He would tell me stories of his basketball dreams and the colleges he was hoping to get accepted into. When Darcy came to work with me for a few hours, Donte would chase her around the produce bins while she screamed and giggled. He was like the big brother she never had. His dad and brother also worked at the store.

After he went off to college, we stayed in touch by phone or through his family and when he would come back home, he would stop into the store to visit all of his old co-workers. I let him know that I may be moving around to other stores or departments, and since I found out that he was majoring in bookkeeping, I wanted him to keep in touch, hopeful that he could work for me someday. There were several other customers and co-workers that have been in my life ever since we met at the grocery store more than 25 years ago. Long-time friendships are a true testament to someone's character. All these people truly helped bring me out of my darkest days and I am so happy to still call all of them family.

STICK WITH THE CLASSIC

During the next year, I began to come to terms with my weight

issues and started jogging two miles a day. I teamed up with two

neighborhood girlfriends and met at the track around the corner

every morning. Darcy would bring her bike and ride while we

jogged and talked. I would also ride my bike to and from work,

which was a couple miles away. I loved being outside when the

weather permitted.

Within 8 months I shrunk down from size 20 to 14, dropping

64 pounds. I looked 10 years younger and finally felt better about

myself and my situation. The girls in the bakery were not calling

me Fatty Patty anymore. The next time Donte came to the store, I

was working up front as a cashier. He walked right past me

without recognizing me at all. First, I laughed, then I yelled to

him, and as he turned around his jaw dropped in disbelief. He

came over and hugged me, saying he could not get over how

different I looked. We caught up quickly on his antics in college, his basketball, and girlfriends, and then he gave me his new number and told me to keep in touch. He had grown and matured so much; he totally went from a teen to a man. I was so proud of him. He introduced me to his girlfriend that he met at college. She was quiet, shy, and sweet. I nicknamed her "Pretty Girl." They lived nearby, so I would run into them every now and then. He eventually broke up with her and found himself a wonderful wife, beautiful inside and out. She truly is his match, and I was so happy for them. I consider them my little family—they now have two children, and we still keep in touch regularly for birthday celebrations and cake deliveries when needed.

A friend from church had approached me about starting a new multi-level marketing sales business. Although I was not really interested in the sales or the products, I did get hooked on the learning part of the program, where you listen to tapes and read inspirational books. This gave me even more desire to get into my own business and propelled me forward with a giant thrust of energy, the new fresh ingredients I needed to make this next batch work. It was time for a new recipe.

I felt confident in my abilities and in my new body. Things were going well for Darcy and me. Her father, who had a new girlfriend, was staying clean from the drugs and he kept Darcy on weekends to keep their relationship strong. Every now and then on the weekends I would grab one of my friends and head out to the local night club for some fun line dancing and flirting. I dated a few men, some I cannot remember, some have stayed good friends over all these years, but nothing more. Ronny, his girlfriend, and I spoke occasionally when it came to matters of Darcy, but I otherwise didn't care to be friends with them, although his girlfriend tried hard to be in my face and in my business. We made an agreement for custody and wrote it up and signed it (unlike last time with Lexi) and we stuck to it. We also had a lawyer draw up divorce papers and quietly let that transpire, so it seemed all was good. The ingredients of the new recipe were in the mix, stirred and ready to pour, when POW!!! — the batter splashed up into my face!!

WHAT A MESS

Before they got married, Ronny's new girlfriend desperately wanted a child and had the nerve to try and TAKE mine. BEEN THERE, NOT AGAIN! One day, Darcy, about 8 years old, was growing up, making friends, excelling in school, and wanted to go outside to play. Because of what I went through with Lexi, I was more protective of Darcy. Usually cautious, I relented and gave her permission to go play no farther than up the street to the mailbox where I could see her, and she could hear me when I called. About an hour later, I called her, no answer, no running footsteps in response to my call. So, I walked to the mailbox, and did not get an answer when again I called her name. I was concerned and angry! She was probably at her girlfriend's house up the street but that wasn't the deal. As mothers sometimes do, I waited to see just how long it would take and how much yelling I had to do for her to get back to where she should have been. After a few minutes of walking farther up the street, and calling out her name, she appeared from the back yard of someone's house.

When she saw the look on my face, she knew she was in deep doo-doo. She came running, crying, and saying she was sorry. As mothers know, this act was not going to work and as some mothers do, I spanked her butt from the mailbox, from where she was not to go past, all the way down the street to our house. It hurt my hand more than it hurt her butt.

Relieved that I found her and not as angry, I did my best to explain my reaction to her. I could see she did not understand, her only understanding was that her butt hurt. The next day, she went to her father's house for her scheduled weekend visit. Two days later, first thing Monday morning, to my surprise, social workers from Child Protective Services showed up at my door. I asked them what they wanted and was told my daughter was being interrogated by the police at school and I was not allowed on the property to get her.

Being a Christian did not stop me from thinking, "What the %$@#?" I demanded to know what brought this on and was told that my ex-husband's girlfriend had taken my daughter to a city hospital showing the Emergency Room doctor what she thought was a bruise on Darcy's upper backside claiming I had beaten her. She was trying to get me in trouble for child abuse so Ronny could get custody of Darcy. "Ditzy" girlfriend did not know what she saw was Darcy's birthmark.

By now I was ready to explode, wondering how someone with a child not their own, or even related to them, could get an emergency examination with no personal information on the child, or a parent present to give his or her permission. I made sure CPS staff had the facts they needed regarding the incident. I did not "beat" my child but did spank her, leaving no bruises. I went to the hospital and demanded to see the attending doctor, as well as those responsible for allowing this woman to take my child into a closed exam room, all the while thinking of a lawsuit for improper handling of the situation.

I proceeded to the school after CPS left, despite being told I should not go. The principal met me on the corner of the property.

Although the principal was polite, she informed me that I could not come on school property until the investigation was over. This could not be happening! How could it be legal for a parent not to be with their child while they were in a room with the police? Who was in there with her? What were they doing to her? What kind of questions were they asking? What were they trying to insinuate? One thing I was certain of, my baby girl was scared, and I was totally pissed off.

Upset and with no answers, I returned home to find another social worker from CPS waiting to question me about my disciplinary methods. I asked her if she had any children of her own? She said, "No."

Check me if I am wrong, but how can a social worker without parenting experiences question my discipline practices? Unless you have walked at least a half mile in the shoes of a parent, guardian or grandparent, your reference is book knowledge and second-hand knowledge.

I told "Ms. Social Worker" that if the case was not dropped by the next day, since the examination showed no bruises but a birthmark, I would be on national news and Oprah, as a parent unjustly accused of "beating" her child, which was not the case. I would have the entire CPS, school system, and police department in an uproar. I was going to bring charges against them and include the hospital for examining my child without my permission. For Ronny's girlfriend to drive Darcy, 35 miles to a city hospital instead of taking her to the county hospital right around the corner from their home was an intentional plan. Girlfriend knew the city hospital staff would call CPS in a heartbeat and that penalties for child abuse were stiffer in the city than in the county. Ronny was called to come pick Darcy up from school and she stayed with him until the next day.

The next day, the situation ended just as abruptly as it started. A document was delivered to my house stating that all alleged charges had been dropped because the investigation did not substantiate child abuse. I was cleared of something I should never have been suspected of and took the paperwork to the principal to clear the accusations. For God's sake I was the PTA president, and we know that would not have gone over well.

I was allowed to continue as PTA president without incident. As for my Ex's girlfriend, I handled that differently.

I dropped Darcy off at her father's house that following weekend as scheduled, acting as though nothing had happened. I had not heard from the girlfriend until she arrived at my house bringing Darcy home from her visit. Darcy exited the car, ran over, and hugged me, as happy to see me as I was her. I immediately, told her to go up to her room and shut her door.

When I walked out of my front door toward the car, Ex's Girlfriend got out of her car and started walking toward me smiling as if she had done nothing! WRONG. I stepped out of my Christianity, ripped into her verbally but decided to listen to my good angel and not beat her down. In my clenched teeth growling voice, I told her to NEVER set foot on my property again and to NEVER pull any more bull using my daughter. Lastly, I warned her if she EVER took my child to any hospital or sought medical care without my approval, consent, or knowledge, unless the situation bordered on life and death, she would not like the consequences. I did not give her any opportunity to respond, and she could see and hear from my tone that she better not. She ran to her car and drove off. She must have stopped and called Mr. Ex right away because my phone started ringing as soon as I got in the house. I knew it was him before I picked up the phone. He asked me what I did to her and I told him, "Not a damn thing and you both ought to be glad I didn't, considering what I wanted to do." I told him I hoped she understood that she is NEVER to interfere with me and my child EVER again. Child Protective Services sent me a letter the next day saying that I was probably one of the best role models in the community. What? I am sure it was to cover their butts; too little too late.

CLEAN UP AND KEEP GOING

During the next year, I dated some nice men, but mostly stayed to myself, worked constantly, and danced to keep in shape.

One night, I was delivering a cake to a club near my house with no intention to stay and socialize. I was on my way out the door when this guy in a trench coat, wearing a hat and glasses (looking like the Pink Panther) stopped me and of all the lines he could have used, he plainly asked to take me out. I rebuffed him and told him I was not interested. He persisted and since I would not give him my phone number, he gave me his. Months later, I called him out of curiosity, and we arranged to meet at Dunkin' Donuts.

Greyson, whom I met right before my 39th birthday, was a distinguished, handsome grey- bearded gentleman. Sitting and talking for hours, I found myself attracted to him. He was older than the previous men in my life, seemed wiser from his conversation, and was employed...or so I thought. Initially, Greyson and I went on some dates, developing a liking for each other. I remember one date, early on, where we met at the local night club. I was real tan and wearing a white cotton sun dress and strappy sandals. It was still daylight when he met me in the parking lot and as I got out, he was all smiles.

He tried to hug me and fill my ear with all kinds of compliments on how I looked and how he was excited to see me as we walked into the club. The attention was nice, but my guard was up.

There was a football game on, some tables of revelers in the front and some people in the back area dancing. We chose a small table up front and he went to get some drinks. I noticed a few girls all into the game at the table in front of us. They were loud and riled up over some of the plays. I could tell some of the men in the room were getting excited by the girls. I think they were just doing it to get free drinks. I minded my business and when I realized that Greyson was more into the game than talking or our date, I decided to go up to the dance floor to shake my booty to a few songs. People that know me, know I cannot sit still very long. When I came back from the dance floor, Greyson was gone. I took a seat and waited, but nothing. I sat there far too long, looking, and waiting to see where he went or where he would come from. Finally, I went looking for him, feeling like a fool, looking in the men's room, outside in the front and back of the place, in his car, and in the kitchen. No sign of him.

I was so glad that I had driven myself. I was so mad and embarrassed that I grabbed my keys and left immediately, completely humiliated. I only lived about 3 miles away, so I got home fast. As I drove, I told myself, I was fit, fine, fabulous, almost forty, and making boss moves and I was not going to put up with the same stuff I had before.

About an hour later, Greyson called me, wanting to know where I went, can you believe that? HA!! What was he thinking? I asked him where he was and he sounded drunk and was laughing and slurring, saying I was crazy for thinking he had left or had gone off with those girls. REALLY?!! Sounded like a lie to me, so I told him not to call me anymore and I hung up. This time I did not fail to see the red flags.

After a few dry months of not dating or hearing from Greyson, I ran smack into him at a liquor store where I bought lottery tickets. He said hello nicely and I brushed past him with a nonchalant, "How you doin'?" He quickly put down the bottles he was holding and followed me out the door. I told him I was not interested in dating someone I could not trust. He apologized for the date that went wrong and told me he would never lie to me. He truthfully said he was dating a few people but would love to get to know me better and if it worked out then we both would be better for it. I told him I would think about it and call him if I changed my mind, then left. He called almost every other day and left sweet little messages on my answering machine, which I mostly ignored. A few months later, I decided to give him another chance.

We met at Dunkin Donuts again and I told him we were going to start all over as if I never met him before and he agreed. For the next few months, he was very good to me; including me when he was around family and friends, which is a good sign. I met his children, and we all went places together and had good times. I met his mom, to whom he was very close, and we hit it off very quickly. He was a very smart man, very sweet, kind, gentle, and frugal.

I opened my heart, home, family, friends, talents, hopes, and dreams to him, believing that we had a very special relationship. After learning about all my jobs and ways that I was making money, he became instrumental in encouraging me to buy a bakery and launch my own business.

Along the 12-year journey of our relationship, I discovered that he had a need to surround himself with a constellation of women, of which I was only one. He never lied about it, I just assumed that as much as we were together that I was enough. Evidently not. As was a pattern with me, I justified his actions because I enjoyed being with him and the sex was great.

I made compromises and kept silent about his being involved with other women. I rationalized that since I could not be with him all the time because of my jobs, the PTA, and my children, it was understandable that he needed to fill that void.

I think I was still searching and hoping for that once-in-a-lifetime, white picket fence, all-to-myself kind of guy.

I continued to live the "The Cinderella Syndrome," which has yet to manifest and may never. While he lacked the qualities to be my forever exclusive man, his purpose was to show me how to imagine and pursue a better life for myself. He would often say "You are killing yourself for everybody else's bottom line. If you just invest in yourself, you can do the same hard work you are doing now and be doing it for your own bottom line." For me to rely on a man is challenging, after experiencing so many disappointing relationships. It seems it is better for me to be alone and do for myself or hire someone if I need help. I tried to do it all: working hard to support my family, working to keep my body in shape, running two miles daily and riding my bike as my mode of transportation; yet, I still entered my fourth decade single, hanging on to what I had with Greyson, which in reality was just a long-term booty call.

To compensate, I brought enjoyment to my life by mastering other skills like bowling, line dancing, and becoming more productive and efficient at decorating. I would stay up late baking, decorating, and talking to my girlfriends on the phone about Greyson.

They would often tell me to let him go, move on, and stop wasting my time. One of my friends said he was there for a reason, and I should try to figure out what his purpose was in my life. I was not able to give any more time to Greyson than what I was giving, as my schedule was very hectic. I felt bad but I also felt there was something special about him. We eventually drifted apart romantically because of time constraints but have stayed close friends to this day. He is often the first person I seek out when I need any kind of financial or business advice and sometimes just a sounding board as he is very wise and humble and gives me a different perspective on my situations.

???

Have you ever had a quick satisfying 'sexstationship'?

Have you ever had to deal with interference from an ex's new partner?

Have you ever stayed in a toxic relationship just because it was comfortable?

A false witness will not go unpunished, nor will a liar escape."
Proverbs 19:5

CHAPTER 9

ALL IN THE MIX

"Whatever good things we build, end up building us." Jim Rohn

The time was right to launch the business I had slowly been building my entire life without realizing it; time to move the cake baking effort from the sidelines into the main arena. It was time to expand the home-based bakery into a shop. My business at home had grown tremendously and was taking over the house. Boxes and boards were everywhere as well as ingredients. The oven was going non-stop. I was still working at the grocery store, sometimes substitute teaching as well as doing my cakes. I had to slow down from everything I was doing from home, on the side, and just work my one job. Greyson told me to "do the math" whenever I talked about operating a business.

Following his advice to calculate my cost, I realized that with my cakes and simultaneous jobs, I was truly growing everyone else's bottom line. With my cakes, after adding all my costs and subtracting the income I was barely making 100 dollars a week profit.

With his nudging, I began looking for bakeries for sale and found that the bakery where I purchased my baking supplies was on the market. Unbelievable! After negotiating back and forth with the owner's broker, talking with my mother, and assessing my financial situation, I made an offer.

Financially, I was strong from saving quite a bit of money since I worked all the time and never had time to spend it. She accepted the offer, but we agreed on a day later in the month for me to take over. I had to wait for my line of credit loan to come through and I wanted to give my home customers the information about transferring operations to Laurel.

The old owner wanted to introduce me in a more formal fashion to her crew, probably so they would continue to work with me.

After getting the line of credit, I made a commitment to remodel the inside of my home and take a cruise to the Caribbean with my kids. The experience opened our eyes to a whole new world. We had a blast on the cruise, and it was just the right ingredient I needed mentally to prepare myself for the new venture. The line of credit allowed me to do everything I planned to do in the house and put down a deposit on the business. The remodeling left my home looking like a furniture showroom, the sweet aroma of cake baking was replaced by the smell of paint and new wood floors from the hands-on work that we did. I promised myself to never again bake another cake at home. I had totally turned the page and was looking forward to baking everything in my new bakery.

I still remember the joy of giving my grocery store boss my resignation and the news that I had bought a bakery; I was stepping out on my own. I did have one request though; to be able to work on Sundays only, because the benefits were so good and working one day would allow me to keep them. Of course, I was denied. My district manager, who mocked everything I said or did, added that I would never amount to anything and would never succeed on my own. She said I would be begging for my job back within a month. Speak of motivation! Her words shoved me out the door, but not before I told her to "kiss my butt" and that I would never come back.

Within the first year, she heard of my success I had proven from experience that I could successfully operate anything I put my mind on and effort into. All the people who said I would fail have eaten their words. Through the Grace of God, my bank account, and the help of family and friends, in November 2004, The Cake Lady's Place, Inc. was born, keeping the business name Kake Korner so as not to lose customers or confuse people. I may not have had a ring on my finger, but I had a business with my name on it. I now qualified for another statistic, only this time it was a good one: a single woman business owner!!!

SEASONAL FLAVORINGS

During the first several months, the previous owner worked with me to teach me everything necessary to succeed. I invested the work ethic and energy in my own bakery that I prided myself on in working for others over the years.' The universe tested my metal as expected, financially and personally. Having the vision, confidence, and determination to purchase and operate Kake Korner changed my perspective about life and especially myself. My personal life was active but not fulfilling, I only stayed in touch with Greyson when I could; there was simply no time for anyone or anything else. Kake Korner consumed my life, 12-16 hours a day, 7 days a week. For the first 11 years, I ate, slept, and drank Kake Korner. For the first three months, I had to learn everything. One thing Greyson told me before I bought the place was "If you can't do everything in there, you have no business buying it." The previous owner taught me her recipes; the cook taught me the timing of the baking; the decorators taught the finishing. I learned all the paperwork and started implementing changes to bring in more business.

Owning and operating abusiness does not mean you live on Easy Street — it comes with peaks, valleys, and a lot of sacrifice. Because of the business, I did not have the flexibility of spending time doing the things I liked. Everyone thinks that owning a business gives you plenty of money, that you are rich. Believe me, that is not the case.

I lost all my benefits and did not have medical or dental for the first eight years, but by the Grace of God, nothing happened. Besides working, I had to keep up with my parenting responsibilities. I was physically exhausted and mentally drained. Sometimes I spent the night at the shop on a little old cot we had upstairs in the office.

EXPENSIVE FLAVORINGS

I had to deal with the previous owner's clients and assume her contracts for any orders still on the books. Another challenge was getting my clients, who purchased cakes when I baked at home, to come all the way to Laurel, 30 miles away. My customers had some feelings about having to pay increased prices and then drive farther to access my cute little shop.

The former owner, whose product was good but basic, was charging her clients a higher price and charging extra to deliver. I learned the hard way when most of my home customers dropped off. The ones who stayed agreed to pick up their cakes at my house to avoid the drive, but they wanted my recipe, not hers, and I could not change recipes over that quickly, so those few also dropped off.

The business came with a baker and three cake decorators. Their skills were decent but later their true colors showed through once I started making changes. The baker tried to sabotage my business by burning cakes and still sending them to the decorators for finishing. When I got a complaint from a customer, I acted swiftly, took over the baking until I had the recipes down pat and then fired her and continued doing the baking myself. For our corporate accounts, I decided to save time and money and ordered pre-baked cakes like we had at the grocery store. I terminated a couple people, hired a couple, and brought Lexi on board part time to help with the increased sales volume. At age 15, Darcy was drafted to work after school and every weekend. She liked baking and decorating and like her momma, was an adaptive person. She then took over the front end, phones, and paperwork, which freed me up to do whatever else we needed. Another major supporter was my sister, who, as a favor to me did a fantastic job as my bookkeeper for the first 5 years in business. She was heaven sent, as I had no time for paperwork, which is critical to the success of a business. She did not charge a dime for her time and services. She would come all the way across town, more than 40 miles, as often as she could because she was still parenting two girls in high school and college. She was the best, but eventually she was needed back home. She recommended a bookkeeper and accountant to handle the large growing payroll, taxes, and accounts we had accumulated. My friend Donte finally got his chance to be my bookkeeper for a few months until the new company took over. The long journey from past to present also saw frequent turnovers in decorators, cashiers, and front-end people.

The business was growing so fast it was hard to keep up. It seemed like every day I had to make necessary changes to accommodate our customers and staff. We changed the phone system to auto answer and that helped if people listened and followed the message. I also changed the whole order form to my recipe only. For the first few years, the customers battled about which recipe they liked best, but they had no choice at this point, I had to streamline everything. After making the changes and many free samples later, everyone confirmed what I already knew and with my recipe, the business took off!!!

Talk about taking off. During that same year, Lexi had traveled to Costa Rica, which I visited while she was there. She met the man that she eventually married and came back pregnant with my first grandchild. I was so happy and excited about being a grandma, even though I was only 46 years old. I worried if I would be able to be there when the big day arrived. My staff told me they would cover for me depending on when it happened, so I was praying it would happen at a non-busy time.

Well, Murphy laughed at me on that one, as Lexi went

into labor in June during one of the busiest days of graduation and

wedding season. On that day, she called me in the afternoon, and

said she was headed to the hospital. I had two cake deliveries, so I

packed them into the car and headed out to drop off the first one. I

stopped at the hospital and she was only 4 centimeters dilated, so I

delivered the second cake, making it back just in time to see my

granddaughter's birth. I recorded it on a cassette tape and a few

days later,played it for my staff. We all laughed and cried tears of

joy. God sent an angel to earth that day, my beautiful little

granddaughter, perfect in every way.

EXTRA FLAVORING

My hand was in every aspect of the business. I did the baking, decorating,

ordering, handled the money, swept, mopped, washed dishes, and took out

the trash. I prayed and cried every day for something to give, as exhaustion

consumed me. We were open seven days a week and holidays. I had to hire

a night baker to help with the increased orders. My third year in business, I

cut the hours of operation and the days back to only six days a week, then opened a second shop in Clarksville, Md. Quite a few of our affluent customers were coming from that area and continually prompted me to investigate getting a small shop there. We were approached by two ladies who owned a flower shop in a small strip mall that had a huge area and needed to rent some of their spare space. We looked at it and decided on a fair price for the 200 square feet and opened the small kiosk inside their shop for pickups and ordering.

The night baker was extremely helpful with selecting the display cases we needed and helped with setting them up in the new location. He did all the baking in the main shop and sent everything up to Clarksville daily. We were so busy with sales and with managing both sites, I could never take any personal time off. I missed numerous weddings and family reunions as well as when Darcy went to her prom and graduated from high school. Lexi helped Darcy do her makeup and I was able to hire a limo to add to her fun. She ordered her dress online, as I had no time to help her shop.

My mom and sister stepped up for me at her graduation, as of course her school would choose the busiest wedding day of the year to hold the ceremony. The sadness from missing these special times is something that will always linger in my heart. I get emotional every time I think about missing her graduation ceremony. I was so proud of her because she worked hard all by herself, without my help for the whole 4 years of high school. She really wanted me there and said she understood, but we can never go back and do it again, that's the part that hurts. That's where all the glitter and sparkle that people think you have in running a business really comes to light as the sour icing on the cake, not glittery or sweet at all.

My mom, who lived close to the new location in Clarksville, worked a few hours a day for about two years until circumstances caused us to have to close. The floral shop lost its lease, Mom developed an issue with her hearing, which made her unable to help in the shop. Although it was becoming popular with the locals, we had no other option than to shut it down and focus on the main location. Though the circumstances were bad, I think it was heaven sent, the timing was perfect. It happened in November, the weather was turning colder, and the holidays were approaching. I am not one who wants to be on the road going back and forth in the ice and snow. My mother's hearing issue turned into a total loss of hearing, which was something none of us ever expected. When I learned this I was crushed and had sporadic crying spells. Once we would sing in harmony while riding together in the car and suddenly that joy was taken away from us. We could not even talk to each other; she could not hear a thing and could not quite grasp lip reading yet. Months later, she got the Cochlear implant and with limited hearing, could talk to us again, but still no singing. Mom would still come to the main shop to help fold boxes and clean, just to acclimate herself to the new changes in her life. In my heart, she will always hold the title for the best employee ever, and she was free, so that made it even sweeter.

VARIETY IS KEY

Around the 5th year, we were in the throes of the
"CUPCAKE CRAZE" that swept the nation. I needed to find a
way we could use the equipment transferred from the closure of
the Clarksville location, so I knocked down a wall and designed a
specific area for the sale of just cupcakes. When we started with
this product line, we offered a pre-packed package of six assorted
flavors, which included vanilla, chocolate, marble, lemon, red
velvet, and strawberry. We found that customers wanted to select
their own, so we amended the setup. We went from offering eight
varieties to over 25, which now requires one full-time employee.
The new flavors we added were spice, carrot, key lime,
Creamsicle, salted caramel, raspberry, and cookies and crème.
This decision was smart, because today our cupcake sales continue
to grow while other cupcake companies have completely gone out
of business. Seasonally, we change the flavors, which always
brings new customers.

A few months later after all the changes were made, Tina, a beautiful young talented cake decorator from New York came in and applied for a job. After looking at her work and resume, I offered her a job on the spot and asked when she could start. I was stretched thin from helping in every area, behind in all my social media management and updating the website. I was on the verge of giving up, she saved my life and the business. Besides being a great decorator, she was also a photographer and media powerhouse. She totally took over redesigning the website, adding fresh new cake pictures and information, resulting in a flood of new customers. She completely raised the bar at the shop and with the rest of the crew. She freely taught them everything she knew to bring them up to the level we needed to be to bring in more money. They also loved her sweet, vibrant personality and worked much better together. At her insistence, they all entered a national contest of cake decorators. All the girls won prizes, some won a few, Tina won one in every category and was crowned grand champion.

This was another great moment for all of them and Kake Korner, as the local newspaper came and did a big article, bringing even more customers. Tina and her husband were newlyweds and had their hearts set on moving to the Eastern Shore and wanted to start their own bakery there.

Although I knew she would succeed quickly, I also knew what a toll it would take on her life. After we cried about her leaving, and her decision to find someplace to open when she settled, I committed to helping her as much as possible. She found a cute place on Main Street, where I traveled as often as possible to help her learn the flow of baking and order taking. She bought my recipe, set up the shop, bought equipment, bought supplies, and opened her first bakery. Of course, Murphy, had to have his turn in all of this and in the final hours leading to the day before the grand opening, her ovens malfunctioned and all of the sample cupcakes for the customers were lost. She was hysterical and called me right away. I immediately called in two people to help and overnight we baked over 300 cupcakes, iced and boxed them up, then transported them 3 hours away to get there just in time for the grand opening. No one was the wiser. She truly did an excellent job as the business also tested her metal in the first 2 years.

Things went so well that she outgrew her location and moved to a larger shop. She stayed there making impressive cakes until she decided it was time for a family. Her wonderful husband approved of her closing the shop and making cakes from home from time to time but was also ready for his big family to start and grow. I bought some of her equipment and she would still come to my shop on weekends to help with the overflow of orders during graduation and wedding season until she became a full-time mom. Within 3 years, they bought a home and now have had their third child. The Lord has blessed them both, and they are truly two of the most wonderful people I have ever known. I call her my adopted daughter and him my son-in-law and the children my grands — another little adopted family.

She still manages my website, social media, pictures, advertising, and head hunting to this day. She thought it would be a clever idea to create a brand for our products since the name Kake Korner had been around for over 48 years. I thought it was a clever idea, too and perfect timing.

I started by taking down all the old junk on the walls and got rid of everything that was costing money and not making money. I recovered some cost by selling items on eBay. We stopped selling chocolate candy supplies, balloons, and snowballs and cut back to offering only cakes and cupcakes. Darcy and I painted the entire interior of the shop pink, black, and white and laid new floors. I commissioned an international company to design a new logo, which I copyrighted and trademarked right away. All these changes created a sense of "renewal" for me and the crew. The new logo adorned our new uniforms, our business forms, and even decorated the walls. We had new shelves lining the showroom and the decorators went all out to adorn them with gorgeous display cakes that wowed the customers.

They loved the fresh, clean, spacious look.

The cupcake room was transformed into an area with decorated display cases with lights and small trays of cupcakes for a variety of flavor options that they could choose. People loved it!

???

Have you ever had to work with or for family? How did that work out?

Do you know anyone who operates more than one business or location?

Have you ever had to miss an important event because of owning a business? How did you feel?

"Forget the former things; do not dwell in the past. See, I am doing a new thing." Isaiah 43

CHAPTER

COOKIN' WITH GREASE

"When God gives you a new beginning, don't repeat the same old mistakes." plannermkt.com

To take a break after all the renovations and helping Tina, I was able to fulfill a dream I had from the very beginning and that was to take my whole crew on a one-week vacation/convention trip to Las Vegas. After a busy day at the shop, we closed the store, ran to catch the plane, and arrived in Vegas, loaded in the vans I had ordered and were off to the hotel to get into our complimentary suites. Yes, a little gambling on my part throughout the years did pay off. Most of the crew had never been to Vegas, so they had no idea what to expect. There were two bakery conventions that week, which provided my staff with learning experiences and fun. I had planned the whole trip to include some great learning, as well as a trip to the Grand Canyon. Our first night there, we went to the infamous Fremont Street Experience. Talk about having a "freaks come out at night" wild and crazy first-night. We saw men dressed like women and vice-versa and half-naked people just standing there waiting to get their picture taken with strangers. Women with beards and lots of brides in wedding gowns. The vans picked us up and took our drunk selves back to the hotel at 3 a.m. The next day was pool time, massages at the spa, and lots of crazy conversations about the previous night's freak show.

The rest of the week whirled by at warp speed, spending our time at the conventions, taking classes, sightseeing, and taking a tour to the Grand Canyon, which was a once-in-a-lifetime experience for everyone. I can honestly say we all had a memorable time, each sharing their adventures to include the good news that some of them hit the jackpot at the casinos. It was great for morale, and we produced plenty of new ideas for the bakery. How often does a small business owner get to take their whole staff on a week-long vacation 3,000 miles away?

CHECK THE TEMP

Life was moving at a breakneck speed. I often reminisce about all the changes we had made, how we had grown, and all the employees that had come and gone over the first 11 years. On our tenth-year anniversary, we held an open house for all ex-employees, as well as customers and friends. Some of the old crew came in and could not believe the space and the bright beautiful fresh look. Over the years, we have had many guys employed at the shop, all of whom were nicknamed "Boy Wonder." I called them that lovingly, either because I wondered about them or they were absolutely wonderful. Usually, the ones who didn't like the name were the ones who I truly had to wonder about and wonder how they made it through everyday life. The ones that didn't seem to mind were the ones that were truly wonderful and took it as a compliment. My original, first one and only true Boy Wonder (who I did wonder about) still comes back to visit often, thanking me for all my lectures and the mottos that I made him promise to live by.

I truly do not have to wonder about him anymore as he is doing great. He does poetry, rap music, wrote his own book, learned how to drive 18 wheelers, and is making the big bucks now. It's truly a wonderful feeling when you mentor someone and then see them prosper. Words cannot describe that feeling.

Anyone who is considering becoming an entrepreneur should adopt a motto before taking the leap. My number one motto, which truly inspired me in the early years of my working life was, "If it's going to be, It's up to me." Nobody is going to do your work for you and you cannot wait for someone to make your dream happen. I knew if I wanted to see something come to fruition, I had to pray about it and get up and do the work. Greyson used to say, "You are sitting on a gold mine." Meaning, if you get up off your butt and hustle you can make the gold.

I used to say all the time, "If they can do it, then I can do it and if I can do it, then anyone can do it. Read that over again slowly about five times. We see records being broken all the time by people who really set their mind to what they want to accomplish.

You can do it!!! Go for it!!!

ODD FLAVORS

Every day when I drove to work, I would see this old man walking down Route 1. He always appeared clean, sometimes "dressed to the nines," as we would say of anyone who took pride in dressing well. I was curious as to where he was going or coming from during his walks. One day when he walked past the shop while I was loading my van, I stopped him. Not sure if he was homeless, had mental issues, or was just meandering his way somewhere, I yelled out to him, "Hello, would you like some cake slices?" At first, he looked at me with a quizzical expression like, "Are you talking to me?" He hustled over to where I was standing, dressed in his short shorts, cut-off top, and work boots looking like a 75-year-old version of the Village People construction worker. I shook his hand, introduced myself, and we stood and talked for a few minutes. He was 72 years old, fit as a fiddle; surely, from walking a lot, and his name was Terry. He had a great smile and told me he was on his way to work.

I told him he looked so much like my friend Greyson, which intrigued him, then he suddenly turned defensive and insulted when I shared that Greyson had two degrees and was quite wealthy.

This stranger then told me he had three degrees, was formerly a pioneer engineer for NASA, and himself had plenty of money. This is when I questioned his mental stability. After this interaction and because he must have really liked the cake, he began visiting often. Sometimes, he would come to the shop stylishly dressed, carrying flowers in hand like he was trying to date me. Now, I have always liked older men, but NOT that old. I nicknamed him Sunshine because of his great smile, and he would always light up the room whenever he came to visit. We talked a lot and became great friends; even the staff embraced him, which resulted in us eventually calling him Pops. Pops, who was respectful of everyone, would sit for hours while I decorated cakes late into the night, talking about anything and everything that crossed his mind.

He was truly super intelligent. I eventually found out that he *was* a Nasa Pioneer Engineer, but had quit his job due to being passed over too many times by white people of lesser seniority and that he was, in fact homeless, living in a shed on someone's property, eating where and when he could, and washing up at McDonalds, which brought back memories for me. Because of his neat and clean appearance, and how super smart he was, I never would have suspected he was homeless. Pops would love it when my mother, who was the same age, would come to the shop. The fact that Mom was Caucasian, he was Black, did not matter — my dad's strong opinions had not rubbed off on mom.

With similar professional and life experiences, they would talk for hours about the past and the way things were when they were growing up. It was so cute to watch them.

Pops would walk the streets picking up metal and turn it in for money, as this was his job. I convinced him to get a cell phone so that I could stay connected with him in case something happened. During sizzling summer days or during winter blizzards, Pops would come to the shop and sleep upstairs on the cot in the office. He was our security guard when we could not be at the shop, especially during severe weather events. This way, I didn't have to worry about him out in the cold freezing to death or having a heat stroke.

He was appreciative and grateful and would say, "It's a sorry rat that only has one hole to go in," which was a lesson for me. Eventually, I gave him a key to the shop and he would come and go, keeping an eye on things for me so that I could go home and get some rest. Pops never asked for anything except to use my phone every now and then to call his sons who lived out of state on their birthdays or Father's Day. He genuinely loved and missed his family and eventually adopted mine as a surrogate family. The Kake crew enjoyed his visits, andwe were all saddened when Pops died. It was August when he passed in his sleep after being diagnosed with pneumonia earlier that winter from which he never fully recovered. We did not find out until weeks later, when we realized we had not seen him. We called the police, who were able to tell us they had found his body next to his cot located in his shed. It was a sad ending to the sunshine he brought into our lives, and, to this day, we miss him. We believe he still visits us at The Kake Korner, as we feel his spirit in the mix.

EXOTIC FLAVORS

Around our 12th year in business, I decided to close on Sundays, shorten our Saturday hours, and take Mondays off, if I could. I decided to book a trip to Dominican Republic by myself and try to write this book, which I did but needed to get it into some sort of order once I got back. Putting my life on paper was therapeutic. The renewal, relief, and freedom was inexplicable. I remember getting on the plane to return with an enthusiastic sense of accomplishment even though there was still so much to do. I also felt renewed towards the business. After the trip, I encouraged my decorators to enter another state competition.

They didn't want to at first, but when I offered to pay for their materials in exchange for the pieces being used as displays in the showroom, they agreed. Each decorator attended and entered several categories of competition. I was able to go the next day when the judges gave out the awards and was overjoyed to find that my entire crew swept the competition in every category with one of my ladies named the Grand Champion again. Excited, we all screamed and cried at the unbelievable announcement. The next day, I called our local newspaper, which came to the shop a week later to interview the winners, resulting in an impressive write up in the paper and for digital media. My winning ladies were proud of themselves and overjoyed about their victory. Some of them are still collaborating with me, producing even greater award-winning designs. We recently made a replica, first time ever, of St. Mark's Cathedral in Venice, for my cousin's 60th birthday. Once posted, it had over two thousand views on social media within the first day of publishing.

I was also excited about the fantastic news that my second grandchild was on his way. This time the birth was scheduled when there was no need for me to deliver cakes in between contractions. I watched the whole miraculous birth, Yucky but awesome! Over the first few years of my grandchildren's lives, I made as much time as I could to babysit, enjoying every minute of it. My grandson was happy, healthy, and handsome in every way. When my granddaughter was old enough to listen and follow directions, I would bring her to work with me, letting her help in the kitchen. She is so intelligent and adorable, her favorite thing to do was crack the eggs. Now she is 16 and ready to come work for me full time on weekends.

YAY!

RICH FLAVORS

Starting to feel like I had put the writing of my book on the back burner, I finally made the commitment to type out what I was carrying in my head and notes. Unable to work on rewriting and making corrections on my own and again getting caught up in running the business, my dream of sharing my story seemed to be fading. A close friend of mine, Linda, whom I reconnected with after 20 years, offered to help me as a ghost writer and editor for my story , which resulted in this manuscript. The way the pieces fell into place was evidence that God still had his hands on me. She took my scattered notes and shaped them with her elegant style and witty ways onto this masterpiece that I would never have been able to do by myself. She is a true gem and a faithful friend forever.

Getting back on track with finishing my book, I was at work looking through the monthly *Bake* magazine. I noticed while reading, a contest was being held where the requirement was to submit a story telling how, as a bakery owner, you started your career. Excited about the possibility of entering the contest, I thought, "Why not just send in a synopsis of my pending book and hope for the best." So, I sat there, wrote a two-paragraph synopsis, and emailed it to the magazine. Never did I think I would win. Again, only by the grace of God did I receive an email 3 months later informing me that my story had won the $10,000 Grand Prize. OMG!!!

I am sure my screams could be heard 30 miles away. I called my editor, Linda, right away to share the news and we agreed this meant that we needed to finish drafting the book, ASAP. I met with my crew to tell them the fantastic news. After reading the synopsis, they were stunned, like others, who had no idea about my background. It was a snowy November day when the representatives from *Bake* magazine traveled from New Jersey to deliver the $10,000 check. Of course, we posted social media photos showing how excited we were. I promptly deposited the check and talked to the crew about how to spend it. We all agreed the shop needed new refrigerated display cases and some backroom storage. After pricing and planning, we bought what we needed, lined up the workers and set about renovating while we were closed during the Christmas and New Year holidays.

I also took some time to finish renovating the basement of my home and started an AIR BNB business and eventually added a second unit upstairs. Another statistic, serial entrepreneur, minority owner of two businesses. Look at God go!!!

??

Have you ever been hard on someone only to have them come back and thank you?

Have you ever met a stranger that quickly became like family to you?

If you thought your story could help someone else, would you enter a contest or write a book to get it out there?

"Forget the former things; do not dwell in the past. See, I am doing a new thing." Isaiah 43:18

Chapter 11

It's Ready

"Sometimes you have to get away to come back stronger."

Sarah Boshnaq

Thirty years ago, if someone had told me that I would be where I am today, I would have thought them crazy. Each day brings its challenges but with it a new beginning, a new opportunity toward achieving my goals. My team of accomplished decorators, bakers, front-end personnel, and managers have my back to ensure Kake Korner provides premier service and an outstanding product. To me, it is a blessing to have a dedicated family of employees who take pride in the business. In the last few years, having a capable staff that could manage everything allowed me to travel.

FLIP IT OUT

In January of 2018, I embarked on a first time, month-long adventure to Europe. Traveling to nine countries in one month was a fantastic, unbelievable experience where I learned many life lessons. I went because I was invited by my friend Linda to Germany where she would be visiting her sister during the holidays. I felt that if I was going to fly all the way over to the other side of the world, I wanted to get in as many stops as I could in one month. I planned the whole trip and lined it up from Washington, D.C., to Ireland, then Wales, London,

then Germany to meet up with her, Belgium, Paris, Barcelona, Rome, and Greece. The one BIG lesson I learned was to NEVER pack heavy luggage again. I credit my staff, who by taking care of the business while I was gone, contributed to my peace of mind. I was free from the daily grind of the bakery and the Airbnb, as my tenants also took care of everything. The trip was marvelous, I learned so much and the memories will be with me forever.

I had a lot on my mind and had started working on a few projects. I was even thinking about starting a third business in property rental for airline personnel. Always looking for opportunities, I did extensive research, developed a business plan, and initiated buying another house to rent out. At almost 59 years old and 18 of those years at the bakery, I was tired of the daily mix of the bakery and felt like I wanted out of the mixing bowl. I thought about selling Kake Korner and even hired a broker to explore my options and an appraiser to determine its value. I went as far as placing a real estate ad to see if there were any interested buyers. I prayed for God to show me a sign, to let me know what to do or which direction He wanted me to go.

My realtor, who was also my uncle, informed me of the value and potential income I could earn from the house I was considering purchasing. Since he owned several food service businesses, he knew from experience the sacrifices owners make in the food industry and that someday I would want out. My broker said there were a couple of people interested, so I accelerated my praying.

I found myself complaining more everyday as I felt everything at the shop was awful, but mostly, it was my attitude. Things were going great at the shop; I think I was just hopeful that this new business venture would be very lucrative and get me out. Going to church and asking for a Word helped to settle my spirit. I received the Word I prayed for.

Like BAM! The very next day, my landlord came into the shop and asked how everything was going. When I told her, I was thinking about selling the business, she said, "YOU CAN'T, PERIOD! She said, "I'm selling the building, so if you don't buy the building you have to get out!" Mind you, this was March when she said, "By the end of December, everything must be moved out and put back to its original condition!" Well, I almost fell to my knees, like the wind had just been knocked out of me. This meant I could not go anywhere or do anything related to selling and moving on. No one was going to buy a bakery business and then relocate within 8 months. To top it off, within an hour, I received a call from my uncle telling me that the lady selling the house had rejected my offer, wanting more money, which I did not have. Talk about a quick answer. Thank you, Lord.

I shed some tears since I had moved ahead with putting things in place for the new business and looking forward to the career change. I quietly sat down and asked God, "What should I do?" I had a meeting with my staff and let them know I needed time to think about the direction the bakery would go and would be taking a couple of days off to get my bearings and some solid advice. They understood, knowing I was growing weary but hoping to keep their jobs with me or a new owner. I understood at that point that God had a purpose for me to stay where I was, so I stayed still and listened for what was to come next. As the old saying goes, bloom where you are planted.

COOLING DOWN

Church was great that Sunday, especially since the pastor's wife was preaching. She hit the nail on the head with a message that seemed as if she was talking directly to me.

I got the message that even though I had made many sacrifices in 18 years, I also received many blessings. While talking to my broker, he explained the details about lowering the mortgage and building equity if I was to buy the building. This helped me realize it made better sense to stay put. Then Greyson, my wise friend, told me to "do the math." It would be a total win-win if I just stayed a few more years, continued to build the business, and own both the business and the property, giving me more options for retirement.

While praying, I realized I was put into this "sweet ministry" (as my friend Lee Michaels coined it 30 years ago) as my calling. God has allowed me, through my business, to help so many people and causes, both in the community, at church, and in my personal life. Throughout my life, giving to others, organizations, even customers, comes natural to me. God has blessed me to share my story — not only through the magazine article — but with this book and students at local high schools. Sharing my past has opened the eyes and ears of many students to what others may have experienced in their lives.

Hopefully, my presentations plant seeds of compassion to not judge others who they don't know and give them food for thought about life experiences. Some of their responses after hearing my presentation have been emotionally overwhelming. I make my sharing interactive, with a homework assignment to ask their parents to share what experiences they had growing up. The business helped me mature, as well as to take care of my children and now grandchildren. Blessed with an income, loyal employees, and tenants at my Airbnb, I have the support that allows me to explore and travel to places "Lil' Miss Independent" would never have dreamed of.

SWEET GLAZE

After working through our annual winter shutdown over the holidays of 2018, painting, renovating areas, and stocking up on some new products, I decided to book a month-long trip to six countries in Asia for my 60th birthday. One of my friends was going to Japan and Thailand and asked me to join her and of course I did, but again I felt I could not go all that way and come back so soon, so I added four other countries that I traveled alone. This trip was from January 2019, until February 2019. The trip started out great, with a 14-hour flight straight through the night from Dulles airport to Tokyo, Japan. When I landed, it was amazing, confusing, overwhelming, and exhilarating all at the same time. Being alone, in a foreign country, not able to speak the language and not knowing where to go or how to get there is very intimidating and scary. You really must make boss moves and be prepared for anything.

I stayed in Tokyo for four days by myself taking various bus trips to different areas each day. When my friend came, we also went to various places each day and had great fun. It was my 60th birthday and we celebrated! We then flew to Thailand for four days, then Krabi Islands, then the Phi Phi Islands, and back to Bangkok. My friend bid me farewell, as she flew back to Baltimore, and I headed to Singapore.

I landed in one of the most impressive airports ever and the city, Singapore, was even better. Again, I took tours every day and walked for hours and hours, exploring everything I could. Meanwhile, my friend who had returned home was texting me over and over to wear a mask and avoid the new virus going around. COVID -19 had been unleashed from China and I was surrounded by hundreds of Chinese people who had come to Singapore on cruise ships and planes for their annual New Year's celebrations. Of course, most people did not know too much about how it was spreading and the severity of the virus, so there were few precautions in place.

Three days later, when I went back to the airport to go to my next stop in Bali, there were mask mandates, as well as chest screening and temperature taking at every turn. They were very initiative-taking in containing the virus. I landed in Bali, and it was like another world.

They had precautions set up at the airports and by this time, the cruise ships were in full turn around mode, but at the beach in Kuta and on all the excursions I went on, there were no mandates or precautions. I did my best to listen to my friend's advice and stay masked up. Bali was nice, but I wish I would have stayed longer in Singapore. My next stop was Viet Nam. They were in full precaution mode everywhere. My first day there, I took an excursion to Ha Long Bay for an overnight boat trip, which was the best fun ever. With people from all over the country, we had a blast singing karaoke and telling stories of our travels. We started a group page on WhatsApp and keep in touch.

Next stop, The Philippines. The city was nice, but not my favorite. I decided it was time to pamper myself and went for the royal treatment at a day spa. New hair color, cut, manicure, pedicure, and massage. I felt like a new person and looked like one, too. In Manilla, they were in full mask and temperature mode; everywhere you went they would take your temp, even at the 7-11. By this time, they had shut down most of the cruise ships and, in a few cases, some were stranded at the docks. The people could not go on their excursions or go ashore for anything. I kept my mask on and stayed to myself. On my last night there, I went to the huge, beautiful casino, had a scrumptious birthday celebration dinner, ate at the most awesome Italian restaurant ever, and hit 600 dollars on a penny machine before I left. Big Win! Happy birthday to me!!

SOUR ICING

The next morning, I left for the airport early as restrictions were now tight and getting through security took longer. I was headed back to Japan for the return flight. I slept 14 hours straight that next day. I should have tried to stay awake so that I would sleep on the plane, as the 14-hour flight was not comfortable and a lot of people were hacking and blowing their noses, which made me even more uncomfortable. When we landed in Dulles, there were no temperature checks, no masks required, no chest screeners, no quarantine rooms, no social distancing, nothing. I was floored and upset to see this — that America was so far behind on procedures to contain this virus that was killing people. While in Viet Nam, I had purchased 20 handmade cloth masks and brought them back for my crew, as I was sure we would need them,but nothing was in place and this was already a month after the news got out.

I slept for two solid days when I got back home. When I returned to work on Monday, I was happy to see my crew and gave them all the masks, which is when they laughed. I kept mine on as a precaution and told them it was just a matter of time. As I had become accustomed to in my life, feeling the circumstances changing beyond my control, I went into survival mode. I had a meeting with my staff and told them what was happening in the other countries and how they were managing it. I also told them to go out and get stocked up for a long shutdown. I really never spoke the word *pandemic*, I was not trying to scare them, only prepare them. The week went by and the things I spoke of started to happen, so I had another meeting, told them to get cash from their banks and pay what they could on their bills. I wanted to make sure they were taking this virus seriously and to get ready for unemployment. They could not believe what I was saying, but lo and behold, within another week we were shut down.

As a business owner, I had to call all my accounts and let them know I was not going to be paying my bills, and to cut off service till further notice. Then my customers started calling and cancelling all their events one after the other all day long, to the tune of 7,000 dollars' worth of refunds in one week. OMG. I had to keep it together for the sake of my crew, I felt like I could cry at any given moment.

I called the landlord and told her there would be no rent for a while, and I put everyone on unemployment immediately, including myself. As a business owner, I cried for my staff more than for my business. My heart ached about not being able to help them, but I could not do anything, as I was watching my whole business that took years to build, go under within weeks.

What took 18 years of blood, sweat, and tears was dissolving right before my eyes, like sand running through my fingers; I could not do anything to stop it. Our bank account was drained. I was ready to dip into the line of credit or close completely when, thank God, the government came through with some help. Although I think Congress was trying to put a band aid on a big gaping hole, the initial PPP (paycheck protection program) loan that we had to scramble to apply for, forced us to go back into the job, risk our health, and come off unemployment, which was paying us more than what we made. It forced us to do curbside pickup, which is not conducive to our business model. It forced us to work harder for less and I still could not put anything in the bank to save, as there were still people cancelling. I told my daughter I wanted to give up at that point, but I couldn't do that to my employees. After the PPP money ran out, we went back on unemployment and shut down again until things got better.

Unfortunately, because of the time we were shut down and the bank account drained from all the refunds, the damage was done. I had to evaluate each team member and let go of half of my employees. This was the hardest thing I ever had to go through. Not knowing what was coming next, I tried to investigate job options for myself, see about finishing the book, doing speaking calls on Zoom etc. I tried to find jobs for the people I had let go. Instead of staying at home sitting all day, I would go into the shop to bake stuff, do paperwork, and clean, just to keep from losing my mind. I decided in September of 2019 that I had to put up shields and open back up, whether we were allowed to or not, just to save the business; otherwise, I would have had to close for good.

I went in on a Sunday and changed some areas, hung shower curtains and signs, as well as put marks on the floor to keep people 6 feet apart. My crew had to move everything down to one floor instead of two, we have one cook now instead of two, and we cut our hours back to less than we ever had before, but by the Grace of God, we are still open. We now have six employees, including me, instead of 14. We are at one-third of the business we had and a year later, still don't know which way it will go. We are hoping and praying for the best and I am still trying to save for the purchase of the building.

FIX AND EMBELLISH

I am so grateful to still be in business, when so many businesses did not make it. Grateful that I can pay my employees who have been there for me. I NOW KNOW where God wants me to be and what I am supposed to do with this awesome gift He has entrusted with me. I know I will keep going and growing, trying to be a better person to whomever I encounter. My hope is that this story will help, inspire, or guide someone else in whatever way it needs to.

If I, the bullied, beaten, sexually molested child, teen mother, domestic abuse victim, twice-divorced, homeless, bankrupt single parent, entrepreneur without a college education can become a successful single woman owner of two businesses, speaker, and author, can do it, then anyone can do it.

I have been blessed with two beautiful children, two grandchildren, wonderful family and friends, and exceptional health.

Despite the direction my life could have taken, it has always been by the grace of God and the blessings He has poured into my life, that I am where I am today, and that is the true *icing on the cake.*

???

Have you ever traveled overseas?

Do you know any serial entrepreneurs?

Do you know someone, or have you had to deal with the pandemic as a boss?

"People may plan all kinds of things, but the Lord's will is going to be done." Proverbs 19;21

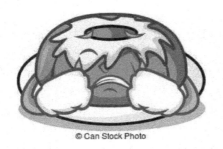

Chapter 12

TEARS FOR TIERS

"In fact, we often prefer predictable, obvious suffering to suffering that may or may not happen at any given time." Kelly

I would be remiss to allow anyone to think that my baking business has

not had its share of memorable accidents, down-right ditzy customers, utter

cake catastrophes, and crazy employees. Some days, we glide through the

day so smoothly that it all seems worth it and other days, I could pull my

hair out, or someone else's for that matter. The drama, like a reality show, is

ever present, we just never know to what degree it may escalate. Many tears

have been shed over my 44 years in the cake business, but I must admit, it has made me grow into the straightforward, no filter, down-to-earth person I am today, and I do not think God would want me any other way, that's why I decided to share some of these crazy stories with you. Enjoy!!!

SPELL CHECK

As all the stories flood back into my memory, I think back to my first embarrassing cake mistake. It was a cake made for my best friend. The cake itself was extremely basic. Nevertheless, I was still proud to present it to her. That is, until she read the writing on top: "To my very best *fiend*." I don't know how such a tiny mistake could make someone feel so small, but I remember the embarrassment well. Luckily, we had a good laugh for a while afterwards and ultimately it taught me to always double check my spelling. We now have two people checking the spelling and sometimes still miss things. Cake decorators need to keep in mind that the most important thing on the cake is the person's name. Also, good handwriting is a must. Poor handwriting alone can ruin the most beautiful cake.

HIPPITY HOPPITY

One year, I had taken a slew of orders for little bunny cakes for the Easter holiday. I had so many, I spent all night baking and decorating, up to my ears in edible bunny fluff. I had to be at work by 5 a.m. the next morning, so I packed my car and off I went. Most of the orders came from people who worked in the building, so they came down for breakfast or lunch, and got their cake. I was feeling great! Everyone absolutely loved their cakes. Unfortunately, the department of health for that county was on the third floor. The lady who inspected the cafeteria got wind of my side business and the fact that I was selling food as a non-licensed vendor, and she came down on me hard and wrote me up. I was pissed. Now, I had to meet people after work in the parking lot and hand them their not-so-fluffy bunnies. The rest of the customers were not happy but understood my dilemma.

Luckily, my recipe was the bomb and no matter if they had received a fluffy or not-so-fluffy cake, they all raved about how good it tasted.

SLICK SPOT

A young Indian couple who needed a large wedding cake contacted me. They wanted an extremely elaborate cake with tiered stands on multiple levels with gold embellishments. I bought all the stands, made the cakes and decorated them perfectly. I was stoked to set up my masterpiece, imagining how the couple and their guests would "ooh and ahh" all night. As I was loading the cake into my car, it started to rain, out of nowhere. I hurried to get the last big layer into my trunk and as I came out of the front door, I slipped right down onto my knee and the cake tumbled into a pine bush while I landed sideways on the porch. "Oh my God!" I yelled.

Somehow, I managed to keep my hand under the cake. I jumped up fast, ran the cake back into my house pulling out a few pine needles, all while trying to keep the blood from running out of the gash on my knee.

I fixed the damaged areas, scurried to the car, loaded it in, and took off down the road like a bat out of hell. I was late and I DO NOT like being late. The bride's father met me in the delivery zone yelling the whole time while I was trying to keep a professional calm face and get the cake inside through the now pouring rain. I was trying to explain that I had an accident and would be set up quickly, but he did not care. I finished the job, without any additional hitch and drove away feeling totally frazzled. Lesson learned, allow at least one extra hour before a wedding starts to deliver and set up, and always pack a first aid kit.

DOUBLE TRIPLE "A" DAY

At one point in time, I had owned two cars, because I believe a woman living on her own should always have a backup. Little did I know, I also needed a backup for the backup. I left the house with 10-year-old Darcy in tow and delivered a handful of cakes back-to-back around the city. I had just pulled up to a stop light when suddenly, my car conked out. I tried every trick I knew to get it back on, but it seemed the car had simply had enough. I had more cakes at my house to deliver so I called Triple A and they towed us home. I quickly loaded my other car with the remaining orders, grabbed one of the neighborhood kids to help, and was off to set up a multi-tiered wedding cake first. We headed down the road and it started to drizzle lightly. I thought, "Seriously?" Rain and cake deliveries are never a good combination. But I still thought we might get to the reception hall before any heavy rainfall. Well, they say when it rains it pours. As I was coasting downhill, about a half-mile away from the hall, the lights started flickering on my dashboard, the radio went out, my wipers stopped, and I COULD NOT BRAKE!!!!! I panicked! Going down a slope in the rain, with no brakes, my child, and another parent's child, other people's cakes, and a wedding cake, I screamed "GOD HELP ME!" This was long before the song "Jesus Take the Wheel!" I told the kids to hold on tight as I turned the wheel slightly and hit the shoulder and then the grass, which slowed me down to a bumpy stop.

Only by the Grace of God did I come to a stop with the kids and the cakes unharmed. But now what? We were still about a quarter mile from the hall, and I had to think fast. So, I got the kids to carry the pillars and poles and I carried two layers of cake as we trotted up the street, over a hill, and into the reception hall. We put the two layers together and then ran back to the car to get the rest. We finished the setup without a moment to spare, as the wedding party was minutes away from being announced into the hall. I allowed myself to breathe the tiniest sigh of relief as we made our way back to the car. I made the second call of the day to Triple A and had them tow that car to a repair shop. I called a friend who was in the catering business and asked to borrow his truck. He picked us up and after driving him back home I delivered the remaining orders. I finally finished around 9 p.m., took his truck back, left his keys under the mat, then

walked with the kids a mile-and-a-half back home in the dark. It was enough time to completely clear my mind and try to convince myself that this was what I wanted to do the rest of my life.

I can feel the anxiety come over me as I relive the details of that day. Lesson: all drivers should have Triple A. I know I will never go without it.

DRIVING THE DOCTOR CRAZY

Speaking of driving cakes, I had employees set out on delivery, only to wreck the cake during travel and bring it back to me. It's funny how they always think it will be easy for me to fix. I was nicknamed the "Cake Doctor" at one point because of the many cake wrecks I had come to rescue. Sometimes, we would barely make it back to the event location in time for the party. We have had employees set up wedding cakes at the wrong reception hall or assemble them on top of stands they were not meant to go on, only to have them topple over and need fixing. Getting a call asking why the wedding cake isn't there yet is one of the worst calls you could ever receive, especially when you know the employee who delivered it had already returned to the shop. We even hired a delivery company at one point to help free up our time by delivering our corporate sheet cakes.

Even though it is one of the easiest products to travel with, they managed to bring countless cakes back to be fixed due to careless driving. One weekend we had made a bunch of strawberry shortcakes for the Embassies in D.C. The delivery company's driver had slammed on his brakes and the strawberries and gel went everywhere. Not a single cake survived. We had to re-do all of them. Honestly, after that incident I was so traumatized that we never made strawberry-shortcakes again, and we fired the delivery company.

FLYING CUPCAKES

Our customers were often no better at traveling with their cakes. One incident I nicknamed Flying Cupcakes, was about a family that came in to order an immensely popular thing called a cupcake cake. This one was very intricate and time consuming. It was totally hand piped with an elaborate array of colors, and it was expensive. The clients came in, all together about six of them, the whole family, looking at and loving the creation they paid so much for. They happily left out with their product and instructions on how to care for it.

In less than 20 minutes, the dad came back into the shop looking upset. Of course, I quickly asked, "Did you forget something? Do you need more cake?" He came over and quietly said that they had put the box on top of the car, all piled in and drove off, totally forgetting the cupcakes were on the roof. OMG. He asked what I could do, as the cupcakes were ruined and in the middle of the road down the street. I'm sure the birds got their sugar high that day. I felt so bad for him and luckily,I had a good decorator on staff that whipped up something very quickly that was close to what he had. He gladly paid again and left, this time with better knowledge of where to put the cake.

Lesson, never put cakes on top of the car and drive off, it will not end well, cupcakes cannot fly.

THE DRUNKEN SHOE

We received a phone order from a man trying to surprise his wife for her birthday. At the time, shoe box cakes with edible flowers, complete with an edible handmade shoe were incredibly popular. The customer informed us he would be sending his neighbor to pick up the surprise. Well, the surprise was on us when the neighbor showed up drunk. We worried that she would never make it home. We did not hear anything back that afternoon and assumed she and the cake had made it safely. The next day, as soon as we opened, the same very ditzy-looking woman showed up at our door, tears streaming down her face with the shoe cake from yesterday in her hand. The cake was a mess. I'll never forget the priceless look on the face of the decorator who made it. She was truly horrified. This woman begged and pleaded for us to re-do it, saying that she would pay anything. She told us that she had gone home, put it on her table, and took a nap (more like passed out in a drunken stupor), forgetting that her four-year-old daughter had a sweet tooth and clearly no one to keep an eye on her. I imagine this little girl excitedly took fingers full of icing and licked them to her little heart's content. For some reason, we took pity on the woman and told her to wait while we worked our magic over the course of an hour, patiently re-doing the whole cake and the shoe.

She could not believe it looked as good as new, and she delightedly paid the $160 we charged. On her way out, she vowed to never get tipsy around a cake and a four-year-old again. We had a good laugh about this one but hoped this woman would get her act together. No lesson here for us, this was strictly on her, but we did learn to make people pay again if they messed it up, it is on our contract now.

DOG GONE CAKE

We had just completed a four-tiered cake for a child's birthday party. It was so heavy, we insisted that it had to be delivered instead of picked up. So, the delivery was made, and the instructions were given to the customer at their home. Shortly after delivery, the customer realized she had forgotten birthday candles and she quickly grabbed her purse and ran out the door. When she got back, she was in shock. In her haste she didn't think about leaving her dog alone in the same room with the cake. He had managed to get up high enough on the counter to lick one entire side of the cake. With a rush of adrenaline, she was able to lift the heavy cake and haul it back to the shop pleading for us to help fix the mess. I will never forget the panicked look on her face as she walked into the store with this half-licked cake in her arms. It took me a little while to fix, as I had to cut away all the pieces the dog had licked, fill it in, and get it back in shape just in time for her party. Lesson: KEEP ALL ANIMALS AWAY FROM THE CAKES! Just like people, they love our cakes!

FRONT-END FIASCOS

There is always drama when it comes to customer service. For one employee, we set up a fake cake purchase just to catch her stealing the money and never ringing it up. Then, we had a customer come in who created drama to take our focus off the ticket with her balance on it long enough for her to shove the ticket in her purse, claim that she paid in full, and while we were looking everywhere for the ticket, she walked out with the cake. We have had customers cuss us out and call us every name in the book, use racial slurs, and threaten lawsuits against us simply because they "thought their cake was going to look different or was going to be bigger," even though they provided the picture and the size. This led us to creating a solid, long-worded contract that we have had to use over and over. We have had employees that stole money, marked tickets paid, some have broken into fights in the showroom in front of customers, and were quickly fired. Sometimes it's like a TV show here.

We can't leave out that we have some of the best customers ever, some have even met here and then married each other. We have had some of the best employees who are like family members. There are so many more stories. I could truly go on for hours. Some funny, some sad, some memorable, and some I wish I could forget. But as they say, the show must go on, and it certainly does at the Kake Korner. Just come in and see for yourself. Maybe we will write another book and call it the Kake Khronicals.

"Count it all joy, my brothers ". *John 9*

Chapter 13

ICING ON THE CAKE

"History is written by the victors, but it's victims who write memoirs."
Will Rogers

The advice I give to anyone going through any part of what I went

through is:

Parents: Parents stay close to your children, watch everyone,

and trust NO ONE, not even relatives. There is evil in this world

waiting for opportunities to enact its desires upon our children,

male, or female, young or old. Stay interactive and in

communication with your sons and daughters to hopefully

prevent them from seeking attention that leads to teenage promiscuity, pregnancy, or experiences that devalue who they were created to be. A 2017 report from the Centers for Disease Control and Prevention found that more than eight million girls experienced rape or intimate partner violence before the age of 18. Our young men and women need the attention, knowledge, and guidance necessary for them to love themselves. Discipline your children, at any age, when necessary, within the guidelines of family rules, in ways that respect their need to express themselves. Communicate your expectations without giving them too many options that can confuse them. Stay with them during their journey, be involved in their life and help them make informed decisions.

Travel: Travel with your children, expose them to places, lifestyles and cultures that offer them options rather than feeling limited in what they can do with their lives. Travel is the best education one can experience and it is cheaper than college. Travel will open their eyes to different races, religions, cultures, experiences, prepare them for life and humble them.

Educate: Actively support your children with their education, to stay in school, and to set goals to pursue a career whether it requires going to college, a trade school, or learning to be the best they can be at whatever he or she dreams of doing. Encourage them to pursue their calling, as we each have God-given gifts and assignments that are only ours to perform. *"Everyone receives a gift. Some people never open it."*

Finances: Stay focused on making and saving as much money as you can. Teach your children the importance of banking and saving and the pitfalls of credit cards. "God bless the child that has his own" rings true. If your thought is that you are saving for a rainy day, there will alwaysbe a rainy day. Do not touch any of your savings. Invest wisely, teach your children investment strategies while they are young. They can become millionaires early or at least be able to do the work that *IS* their passion by starting to save and invest a percentage of their money at an early age.

Family: Young women who want to marry, do a thorough "411" background check on your prospective husband before you take the leap; dig deep, observe their personality and how they react or respond to certain situations, which may give insight to possible abusive behaviors or mental instability. I found reading the book *"Personality Plus"* by Florence Littauer helped me to better understand all people. Another title that blessed me with greater insight, *"The 5 Love Languages."* by Gary Chapman. Avoid any male who does not treat you with respect, dignity, and care. Read, read, read to answer any questions you may have if there is no one with whom you can talk to. If you can, take classes to better understand human behaviors. Divorced or single women moving through broken relationships, **exercise sexual restraint**. Set your standards high so that no jerk will jerk you around having you believe you are the one-and-only when you are only the side chick. Do not waste time or years with anyone who does not have a serious intent to put a ring on your finger within 2 years.

Set a deadline for how long you want to invest in that relationship. You are investing time into your future, so you should expect a return on your investment. Love your family as family, not for what they can do for you or what you can do for them. Family is everything, even when some may seem a little, as young people say, "cray cray." Crazy or not, they are still your blood.

Career: For those with entrepreneurial blood running through their veins, prepare yourself well, do your homework, read, and research what you want to do, access available resources and people, such as SCORE, an organization that offers guidance and support from retired business owners or heads of corporations. Mentors are available to provide expertise. Develop a business plan, work it, and continue to save most of what you earn, if possible, thinking ahead to your retirement.

Always pay yourself first and set up an investment account. Live within your means for what you need, not what you want. Pursue getting your legal brand and trademark early in your venture. Taking short cuts usually results in money loss, do it right the first time. Get a patent attorney, which may cost up front but will save you money and headaches in the end. Smile when you decide to sell your business. You will be branded and well known and be able to get a well-deserved selling price.

Fun: Take a vacation. Do not live to work but work to live a life that rewards you for your effort. Why wait 10 to 12 years in your business before rewarding yourself and your family? I suggest you take a one week rest or vacay every three months to refresh yourself, to bring new ideas to your work and to create loving memories with your family. Be sure to seek out deals and vacation within your means. Don't break the bank every time you go, there are always good deals and check ahead of time with a travel agent to keep their eyes open for you. Truly relax and unplug for a while, you deserve it and need it.

Health: Take care of your health, get the rest your body dictates to be of good mind, body, and spirit in operating your business. Workout often, eat right, and sleep well.

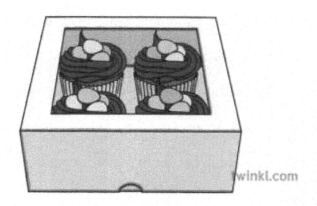

BOX IT UP

The last piece of advice I want to share is to live your life to the fullest as if it is golden, because it is! Live every day to the fullest, take time to be good to yourself, laugh, go dancing, bowling, golfing, go to the beach, attend concerts, visit with family and friends. Write letters to those you have not communicated with, use social media in healthy ways to locate and rekindle relationships or to just say hello. Spend as much time doing the things you enjoy doing or try new things you would like to do. Do not try to please everyone on Earth and do not worry, think, or care about the negativity other people try to pour into your life.

Many people have died too soon without having had experiences outside of working, sleeping, and striving for a lifestyle that adds stress and can be unfulfilling. Make memories. Live responsibly. Love and serve God. Be grateful every day for everything. These are valuable lessons that the pandemic has taught us. Be OK with **everyone** since **their agendas** or plans are **not yours** and **yours** are **not theirs**. Everyone, for better or worse, is here for **THEIR** purpose, to survive, live, and have what **THEY** love. Honesty and integrity are invaluable and will show through your character. "The Golden Rule"encourages us to treat others as we wish to be treated.

So, love **everyone** for whatever they bring to the table, *and hopefully,*

IT WILL BE A BIG SLICE OF THE CAKE LADY'S CAKE!

ENJOY!!!!

Thanks for reading my story. I only hope to inspire someone out there to keep going, even after tragedy or pain, God has a plan for you!!

Please feel free to email me your story or thoughts diane@mylifeinthemix.com and our website Mylifeinthemix.com

Also check out our Facebook page, MY LIFE IN THE MIX and our Instagram page and our original KAKE KORNER. COM   AND CLICK ON OUR FACE BOOK AND INSTAGRAM PAGES AND CHECK OUT OF EDU-CAKE-TIONAL VIDEOS ON YOU TUBE

My first birthday.

Lil' Miss Independent

From "Roach" to prom queen

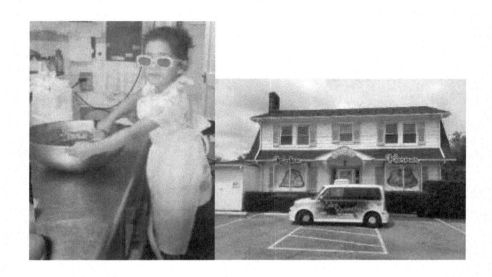

My grand daughter at 5 yrs old. 2. The Kake Korner bldg. and car
3.   The big 10,000 check   4. The huge replica of St. Marks